The Basics of
Buying Property in
Portugal

The Basics of
Buying Property in
Portugal

JUNITA MAREE MOLLER-NIELSEN

Junita Maree's

Printed in Australia.

ISBN-13:   Paperback   978-0-9942398-0-8
           Hardback   978-0-9942398-1-5

Rev. Date: 05/13/2015

Junita Maree's

Website: www.thebasicsofportugal.com
Facebook page: https://www.facebook.com/TheBasicsofPortugal

CONTENTS

Copies of Contracts

About the Author

Junita Maree Moller-Nielsen is an Australian who travelled to Portugal for the first time in 2009. She fell absolutely in love with Portugal so much so that she went back and bought her first property in Figueira da Foz in 2012. *The Basics of Buying Property in Portugal* is her first book.

Acknowledgements

This book is a result of the processes, trials and tribulations I went through during the process of purchasing my Portuguese property.

I wish there had been a book like this available that I could have bought at that time, outlining the basic processes. It would have made things so much easier and helped me to avoid the numerous pitfalls and frustrations that many Portuguese and foreigners experience when purchasing a property in Portugal.

Thanks to my son, Daleth, who experienced this process with me, from the very beginning when I put in my first offer to the owner, to my jubilation after my final offer was accepted.

To all my amigas and amigos from all walks of life, who have been there for me from when I first arrived in Portugal on holiday until now; your friendship and hospitality has been wonderful and will never be forgotten.

To all my friends and family in Australia and all around the world, thank you for being supportive in my journey so far.

Introduction

I first came to Portugal in 2009 to visit my friends; on that first visit I absolutely fell in love with the landscape, lifestyle, the people and the culture of Portugal.

There are many varying landscapes throughout Portugal, from valleys of flowers, olive trees, bushland and farmland, to beautiful beaches along the Atlantic coast.

The Portuguese lifestyle is very simple and in most areas is self-sustaining; they grow their own vegetables, produce olive oil from their olive trees, make wine from home-grown grape vines and breed their own livestock for meat.

A person can live a simple uncomplicated self-sustaining lifestyle in Portugal for a very small cost, compared to Australia and other countries around the world.

I have travelled all over Portugal, from Mirandela - a beautiful picturesque town with a beautiful river in the far north (where my friends Franklin, Helena and Alexandre are from), to Albufeira in the far south.

Oporto was where I first landed in Portugal, where they have the beautiful Douro River and also where my good friends (amigas in Portuguese) Deolinda and Maria Juan are from. It is also where I first tasted "Superbock" (one of the Portuguese beers, Sagres is another) and had "Francesinha" (which is like an un-toasted steak sandwich covered in a mouth watering sauce, not dissimilar to gravy) and where I took my first Portuguese boat ride.

I then travelled onto the Coimbra District, visiting Coimbra city, Mealhada (renowned for having the best roast small pigs in all of

Portugal at Pedro's Restaurant - in any case that's my opinion) and Vacariça.

Following on to Figueira da Foz, where I fell completely in love with the wide white sandy beaches, majestic sunsets, the people and the town itself.

Then on to Lisboa, where I lived in the suburbs, Anjos and Martim Moniz. I travelled all over Lisboa, exploring all the nooks and crannies of this beautiful city, the culture, food and the way of life in the capital city of Portugal.

In my last couple of trips to Portugal, I headed down south to the Faro District in the Algarve, specifically Albufeira and the surrounding areas.

In travelling the vast areas of Portugal, through small villages, towns, main cities, mountains and beachside towns, the one place which reminded me of Queensland in Australia was Figueira da Foz. The lifestyle here is similar to that of a Queenslander, which is why I fell in love with Figueira da Foz.

It is so clean, well kept, peaceful and to me invigorating, because of all the activities one can pursue there. So, after researching many areas of Portugal, I finally decided where I felt most at home and then proceeded to buy my first property. I began the purchasing process in October 2011 and it officially ended in January 2012 when it was transferred into my name; I finally became an owner of a Portuguese property.

In Portugal, whether you are interested in buying property for personal, recreational, rental or business use, there is a wide range of properties on offer that are quite affordable.

It all depends on your reasons for purchasing a property in Portugal. For me personally, the property I bought is a three storey building that

I am currently converting into a guest house/hostel, with a couple of shops on the ground floor and a bar.

In total I have estimated it should cost a total of 160,000 € (euros). After all the renovations are done, my property should be worth at least an estimated 600,000 €. Not bad for a 160,000 € investment.

I spoke to a great deal of people, both Portuguese and foreigners, regarding the purchase of a property in Portugal, prior to buying my property. I found out that it was a major complicated process for some, so I thought I would write a book on the procedures of buying a property in Portugal, to help everyone, both Portuguese and foreigners.

In this book I will try to make it very simple and basic, compiling all the information I have researched and gathered, together with all the processes I went through in purchasing my property.

This book, I hope, will be a guide that will show you the most basic, simple process to purchase a property in Portugal and to help guide you through a hassle free transaction process.

Purchasing a property is one of the most important decisions a person can make in their lifetime, whether it be their first, second or even their tenth property.

In purchasing a Portuguese property, it is your choice what you wish to do with it; keep it for personal use, rent it out, use it as a vacation home or, like myself, renovate and turn it into a guest house or hostel. Your choices are limitless.

I hope this book makes it easier for you to purchase a property in Portugal. Remember, this is not designed to be investment or financial advice - it is just a simple guideline that I hope will help you in your endeavours.

PORTUGAL

Portugal is one of the oldest nations in Europe, having established its continental frontier, as it is set today, in 1297. Portugal has been an independent Kingdom since 1143, when D. Afonso Henriques rebelled against his mother to wrestle the Condado Portucalense away from the Kingdom of Leon.

Portugal is situated on the west side of the Iberian Peninsula, ideally positioned between Spain and the Atlantic Ocean. Its geographic location along the Atlantic coastline is the reason why Portugal quickly became an ocean-bound country, setting the stage for centuries of sea adventure and discoveries.

1415 was the year that set the tone for centuries to come. Under the guidance of Prince Henry "The Navigator", the Portuguese set sail on epic voyages that would make them the first to discover the ocean routes to India, Brazil, China and Japan, while at the same time founding settlements on both African coasts.

Traces of this worldwide historic presence may be seen as trademarks of the Portuguese culture. The Portuguese language became one of the most widely spoken in the world, and the Portuguese people were privileged for being exposed to so many different civilizations. The vast monumental, artistic and archaeological heritage witnesses not only the 850 years of history of encounters with distant cultures, but also the presence in the territory of more ancient peoples (Celts, Suevians, Visigoths, Romans and Arabs).

Portugal's natural advantages, as a sunny country with such diverse geographic features, have turned the country into a chosen destination for many holidaymakers, an ideal place for practising water sports and playing golf, offering modern tourism facilities and quaint and personalised means of accommodation, such as Solares de Portugal (privately owned homes, ranging from wonderful farm houses to manor houses) and luxury and charm hotels located in castles, old monasteries and manor houses, known as Pousadas of Portugal.

As outlined on the Living in Portugal website:

http://www.livinginportugal.com/en/where-to-buy/#sthash. oHBpEfL3.dpuf

STEP 1

ORGANISE FINANCE TO PURCHASE A PROPERTY

There are various options available for you to purchase a property

I chose to buy a property in Portugal, not only because I fell in love with the country, but also because I saw its untapped potential.

Over the last twenty or so years, I have read hundreds of books on building financial wealth through real estate investments. I am sure many of you have read similar books by the likes of Napoleon Hill, Robert T. Kiyosaki, Donald Trump, Zig Ziglar, Warren Buffet, to name but a few.

I believe that anyone can apply all they have learnt, either by researching or previous investments in their own country or other countries; I am sure they will agree that Portugal is an untapped market just waiting for foreign investors.

Listed below are some options that may be available to you:

1. Invest your own personal finances.
2. Apply for a mortgage with a Portuguese bank.
3. Apply for a mortgage in your own country of residence.
4. Make a contract with the seller to make a certain amount of payments over a set period of time.
5. Swap your own personal real estate or other property you own outright (for example: a vehicle, caravan, shares, boat etc.) for the property in question.
6. A Rent/Buy contract is where you can rent the property for a certain amount of money for a certain period of time and the money can be used as a down payment or deposit until you qualify for a bank loan or are able to raise the money in another way to purchase the property.
7. The property owner can organise a loan for you, where you make the repayments over a certain period of time, but bear in mind that if you are late or behind with your repayments, the property will revert back to the original owner, who also keeps any payments you have already made.

The cheapest land I found for sale in Portugal was a 50 square metre plot, full of Eucalyptus trees (native to Australia), listed for sale for only 100 €.

The cheapest house I found was a 25 square metre house with a 1,000 square metre plot of land (just down the road from the house), for 2,000 €.

Recently I just missed out on a six bedroom, three storey house listed on *www.olx.pt* for 5,000 €. With properties this cheap, one will always be able to make a return on their investment.

STEP 2

RESEARCH THE COUNTRY'S LANDSCAPE

Know the following;

- *Where you wish to live*
- *What the purpose is for the property*
- *Type of property*
- *Beach property*
- *Farmland*
- *Mountains landscape*
- *Village lifestyle*
- *Bush lifestyle*
- *City lifestyle*
- *Rivers, streams, ocean*
- *Vacation property*

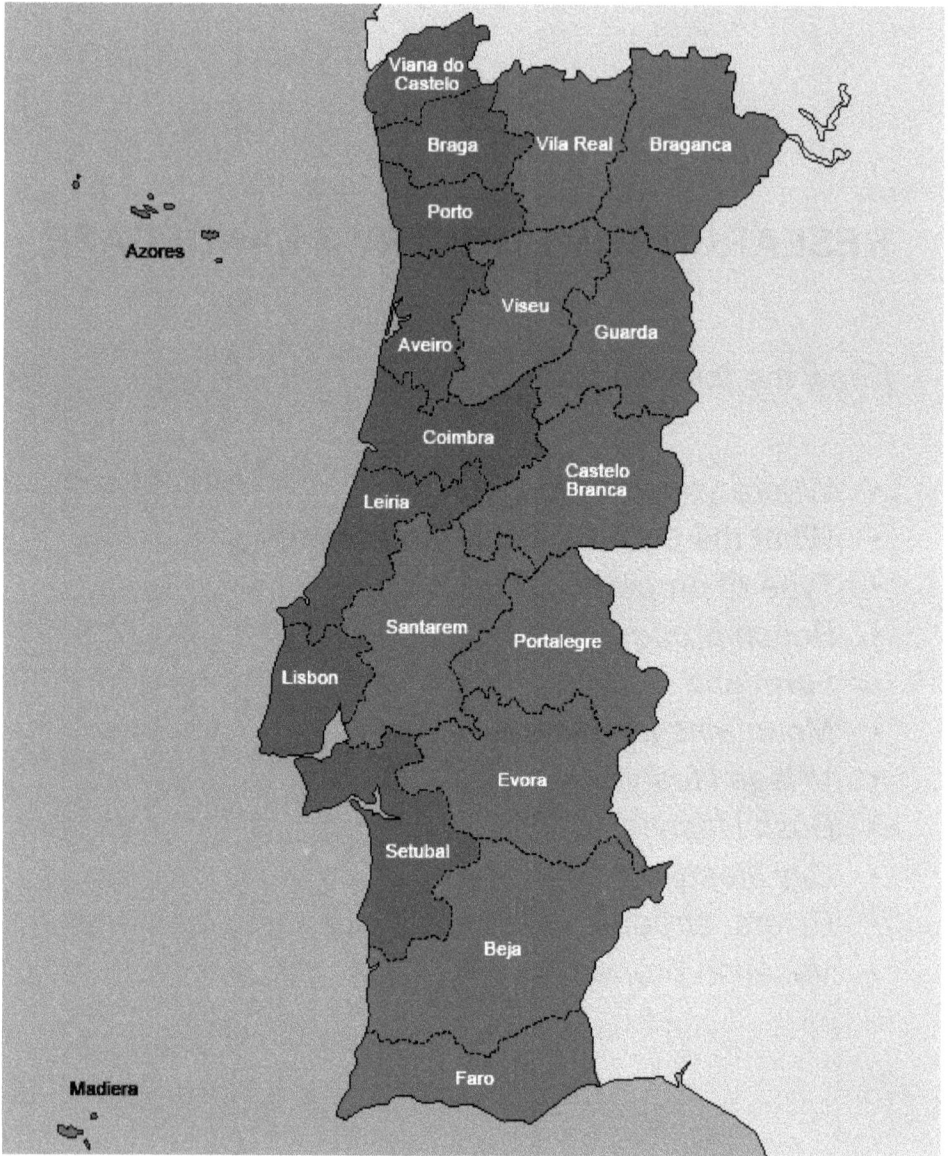

A map of all the Districts in Portugal

MAIN CITIES, TOWNS, VILLAGES AND ISLANDS OF PORTUGAL

Around Lisbon and Tagus Valley
Alcobaça
Arrábida
Azeitáo
Batalha
Cascais
Ericeira
Estoril
Fatima
Leiria
Mafra
Nazaré
Obidos
Palmela
Peniche
Queluz
Santarém
Sesimbra
Setubal
Sintra
Tomar

Alentejo
Beja
Castelo de Vide
Elvas
Estremoz
Evora

Marvão
Mértola
Monsaraz
Vila Viçosa

Algarve
Albufeira
Faro
Lagos
Sagres
Silves
Tavira
Vila Real de Santo António
Vilamoura

Beiras (Central Portugal)
Aveiro
Belmonte
Buçaco
Coimbra
Conimbriga
Figueira da Foz
Guarda
Monsanto
Piodão
Serra da Estrela
Viseu

Porto and Douro
Amarante
Lamego
Porto

Minho
Barcelos
Braga
Gerês National Park
Guimarães
Ponte de Lima
Ponte de Barca
Viana do Castelo

Tras-os-Montes
Bragança
Chaves
Vila Real

The Islands
Azores
Madeira

A BREAKDOWN OF ALL 18 DISTRICTS OF MAINLAND PORTUGAL INCLUDING THE NUMBER OF MUNICIPALITIES, PARISHES, PROVINCES AND REGIONS

District	Municipalities	Parishes	Province of 1936	Region
Aveiro	19	208	Beira Litoral Province + Douro Litoral Province	Norte, Centro
Beja	14	100	Baixo Alentejo	Alentejo
Braga	14	515	Minho	Norte
Bragança	12	299	Trás-os-Montes e Alto Douro Province	Norte
Castelo Branco	11	160	Beira Baixa Province	Centro
Coimbra	17	209	Beira Baixa Province, Beira Litoral	Centro
Évora	14	91	Alto Alentejo	Alentejo
Faro	16	84	Algarve Province	Algarve
Guarda	14	336	Beira Alta Province (partly Trás-os-Montes e Alto Douro)	Centro (partly Norte, only Vila Nova de Foz Côa)
Leiria	16	148	Beira Litoral Province, Estremadura	Centro
Lisbon	16	226	Estremadura (partly Ribatejo)	Lisbon (partly Alentejo)
Portalegre	15	86	Alto Alentejo Province (partly Ribatejo)	Alentejo
Porto	18	383	Douro Litoral Province	Norte
Santarém	21	193	Ribatejo Province (partly Beira Baixa and Beira Litoral)	Centro, Alentejo
Setúbal	13	82	Estremadura Province, Baixo Alentejo Province	Lisbon, Alentejo
Viana do Castelo	10	290	Minho	Norte
Vila Real	14	268	Trás-os-Montes e Alto Douro	Norte
Viseu	24	372	Beira Alta, (partly Douro Litoral)	Centro, Norte

You can further research each individual area, to see where you would prefer to purchase a property, as they are all different and with many diverse landscapes.

If you refer to the following website address:

http://www.livinginportugal.com/en/where-to-buy/#sthash. oHBpEfL3.dpuf,

this outlines each of the regions as listed below:

Porto and the North of Portugal

Porto and the north is a region where history, culture and nature are perfectly combined, making it a unique destination. Religious heritage, modern architecture, natural parts, hospitality, gastronomy and the prized Port wine are all major attractions in this region.

Centre of Portugal

The centre of Portugal is a region of contrasts, where visitors can discover picturesque towns along the coast or take a tour through historical villages, such as the villages of Xisto, or to the border castles, where Portuguese customs, traditions and fine cuisine are still preserved.

Lisbon Region

Lisbon is a cosmopolitan city; it is one of the most fashionable European capitals, as well as the name of a region that has a lot to offer: imposing monuments, natural parks and a wide range of golf courses. It is close to the Estoril coast, the romantic towns of Sintra, Óbidos and Tomar, sites of touristic and cultural interest, as well as The Sanctuary of Fátima, one of the most important shrines to the Virgin Mary in the world.

Alentejo

Plains of wild flowers, tranquil lakes, welcoming towns and villages and horizons as far as the eye can see. Here, visitors can discover a megalithic ancestral heritage and vestiges of Roman, Moorish and Jewish culture, the largest artificial lake in Europe, the best place in the world for viewing the sky (designated by UNESCO) and one of the best preserved stretches of coastline, with many kilometres of white sandy beaches.

Algarve

On the Algarve, internationally one of the best known Portuguese destinations, you can find plenty of sunshine, a wide range of beaches, water sports, spas and thalassotherapy, plenty of entertainment and some of the best golf courses in the world. Natural reserves, cultural heritage linked to maritime history and the Portuguese discoveries, and local cuisine heavily geared towards fish and seafood, are just some aspects of the diversity that this region has to offer.

Madeira

The Atlantic islands of Madeira and Porto Santo, with their subtropical climate, are well-known for their natural beauty that encourages visitors to pursue open-air activities and seek wellbeing. Discover the heritage and culture related to the Portuguese discoveries and Madeira wine, as well as the festivities that are one of its greatest attractions.

Azores

The nine islands of the Azores are an ideal destination for rest, relaxation and getting in touch with nature. Right in the middle of the Atlantic Ocean, the islands are a fine place for diving, rock-pooling, hiking and bird-spotting, but also for enjoying extremely valuable cultural heritage.

STEP 3

IDENTIFY REAL ESTATE AGENCIES

Know the main local real estate agencies and their sites – this can save you thousands of dollars in purchasing your property.

Once you have become familiar with the map of Portugal, either by travelling there or via the internet, you can then move to the next stage, researching the various real estate sites on the internet and surfing the web for properties for sale in Portugal.

The real estate agencies I personally used are as follows;

- *www.era.pt*
- *www.remax.pt*
- *www.imovirtual.pt*
- *www.casasapo.pt*
- *www.solimobiliaria.pt*

When using *www.casosapo.pt*, *www.solimobiliaria.pt* and *www. imovirtual.pt*, you are able to see all the smaller real estate agency listings from all over Portugal.

The five listed above are the main real estate agencies in Portugal; Era was the main one, where I was able to find my beautiful property in Figueira da Foz.

If you are a foreigner, please remember to be patient, as it may take some time for them to reply to you; my experience has been roughly about 4-7 days, as I believe they are making sure they have someone who is fluent in English to correspond.

For Portuguese citizens or foreign residents who are fluent in Portuguese, it shouldn't take long at all.

Another website that is used by property owners as well as real estate agents is *www.olx.pt;* there are thousands of properties of all types for sale on this site. I found many interesting properties listed here. *www. olx.pt* is similar to, if not the same as, the ebay websites that Australia and America use.

The sites I have listed should enable you to find some very affordable properties, such as land, mobile homes, apartments, houses, buildings and shops to name a few.

www.green-acres.pt is the one mostly used by foreigners when searching for overseas properties.

I could give many internet sites for real estate agencies representing Portugal but, like the title of the book says "The Basics in buying a Property in Portugal", I really do wish to keep it basic. The easiest and most affordable properties can be found through the sites listed above and I have found these to be the most efficient and effective ways of searching for a property in Portugal.

Most of the real estate sites are available in a number of languages; if necessary you can use *https://translate.google.com/* to translate if you are unable to find your own language.

Once you have identified a property you like, have seen it in person and you can imagine yourself living there, you can move on to the next stage if you are ready to make an offer on the property.

STEP 4

GOVERNMENT AUCTIONS

*Portugal Financas have a website
where they conduct government auctions online.*

I have also used the site from the Portugal Financas, which is a government department where owners have failed to pay their rates, properties have been left to the state or there is no family member to claim the property after the death of the owner; the government takes ownership and auctions off the property to recover taxes, etc.

http://www.e-financas.gov.pt/vendas/home.action

If you have identified a property you like on this site, you can proceed on your own if you are Portuguese. If you are a foreigner, it may be easier to find someone fluent in Portuguese or an advogado (lawyer) that can advise you on how to go about bidding, and securing the property if you make the winning bid.

Basically, there are three options to purchase a property from "Financas":

Option 1   Online auction

Option 2   A closed letter

Option 3   Private negotiation

Buying a property on a government auction for a fraction of the value price sounds very tempting, but before you participate in a "Financas" property auction, there are a few things you need to know:

Every property has a curator, a private person, a real estate officer or other entity. Their responsibility is to show the property during a specified period of time before the auction. Their name and contact information is shown on the webpage of the auction.

The auction will last for a period of fifteen (15) days and the starting price will be 70% of the value of the property. If there are no bids during that period, the online auction will be over.

For a period up to twenty (20) days after the online auction is closed, the Financas will accept closed letter proposals with a starting bid price of 50% (see a copy of a closed letter proposal at the end of this chapter).

If, after the second period there are still no proposals, the property will be auctioned again through the normal online system, but this time the auction will not have a minimum starting bid price. It can be sold for as little as one (1) euro. YES, IT IS TRUE!! A PROPERTY CAN BE BOUGHT FOR ONE (1) EURO.

The purchase of the property will be subject to the payment of taxes. When you bid, remember that this is the price without taxes. At the time of the purchase of the property you are required to pay the two (2) following taxes:

- **Imposto Municipal sobre Transmissão Onerosa de Imóveis**

In English, this basically means Municipal taxes (city/council taxes/rates) on transferring property

- **Imposto do Selo**

In English - Stamp Duty

You can apply for the auction online or through a closed letter proposal. I prefer **Option 1** as you can easily follow up the result online.

A closed auction means you have no access to the other proposals and the result will only be known at the end of the auction. The results will then be published online for thirty (30) days.

If you win the auction, you have to pay one third (1/3) of the value immediately and the remaining two thirds (2/3) within fifteen (15) days.

If the total value of the property exceeds 51,000 € you can ask for an extension to pay the two thirds (2/3) within an eight (8) month period.

There is no contract between you and the Financas. Once you place a bid, you will be committing to the purchase of the property, as regulated by Portuguese law.

Once you have paid the full amount for the property, the Financas will give you a document called **"Auto de Adjudicacao"**, which basically works as a bill of sale and transfers the ownership of the property to you.

At this stage the property is still not yours! There is a period of time (depending on the legal process) during which other parties may oppose the transfer of ownership of the property to you, such as banks, disgruntled spouses or family members etc.

After this period has ended and assuming no-one has opposed the transfer, the Financas will give you a legal document that cancels all mortgages, releasing the property to be registered under your name.

Normally the purchase of a property requires a contract "Escritura" between the seller and buyer, which has to be made at the Notário. The scenario mentioned above is the only situation in which there is no "Escritura" or contract of any sort. It has been regulated this way to make the transfer of these properties simpler and to reduce costs for the future owner.

Two (2) documents (Bill of Sale & Cancellation of all Mortgages) should be given to you from the Financas, both of which you need to then take to the Conservatória do Registo Predial (in English – Certificate from the Land Registry). This is where you can finally register the property under your name as the sole owner of the property.

Please remember that the properties listed may need to be fully renovated or completely demolished and rebuilt. You may be able to purchase a property at a cheap price, but bear in mind it may have extra costs, or hidden costs due to the property needing to be renovated or completely rebuilt.

Before purchasing any property, check the property's history and legal status

For this, you need to see the **"Certidao do Registo Predial".** This is a document that contains the full history of the property. Usually, the curator has a hard copy of this document.

You can also get a copy from the "Conservatória do Registo Predial", in the region where you wish to buy the property.

This is a very important procedure - any purchaser should always do a check on the history of the property and its current owners. In Portugal, it is common for a small percentage of the building to be owned by someone else, a company, or the property could have several bank mortgages, liens or even pending legal action against the owner.

In addition, the property could be currently rented out to someone and you may not find out about it until after you purchase the property. In Portugal, all tenants who have a rental contract in place are legally protected by that contract.

Copy of Contract: Closed Proposal in Portuguese.
(Dados do comprador: Nome, morada, contribuinte e contactos)

Data: _____

ASSUNTO: PROC. No. _____
TRIBUNAL JUDICIAL DE _____
INSOLVENTE: _____

Excellencies,

Vimos por este meio apresentar a nossa proposta para aquisição dos bens a seguir identificados referente ao processo supra identificado:

Verba No: _____
Total: _____

Informamos V. Exas. que tomámos conhecimento do regulamento, não tendo nada a opor às condições de venda.

Sem mais,

Atenciosamente,

_____

Copy of Contract: Closed Proposal in English.
(Buyer Information: name, address, VAT number, phone and email)

Date: _____

SUBJECT: PROC. No.   _____
COURT OF _____
INSOLVENT: _____

Excellencies,

    We hereby submit our proposal to the acquisition of the assets below identified, referring to the above identified process:

Amount: _____
Total: _____

    We inform Your Excellency that we understand the terms, having nothing to oppose to the selling conditions.

No further,

Sincerely,

_____

STEP 5

BANK PROPERTIES

Bank auctions are another way to find bargains. The auction is usually conducted in the standard format. Normally it takes place with everyone present in a room, each holding a number card, in an open auction. There are some auctioneers that organise online auctions, but this is less common.

One example:

- *http://www.uon-imobiliaria.pt/imobiliario.aspx?lang=EN*

Each auction has its own rules and these are set by the banking institution or the auctioneer commissioned to conduct the auction. It is imperative that you consult the regulations of each auction before signing any contracts or papers, so that you completely understand the regulations prior to making a bid.

Auctions are usually announced on the websites of the banks and also by the auctioneers or real estate agents.

Some examples:

Caixa Geral de Depósitos (Bank)

- *http://www.caixaimobiliario.pt/leiloes/*

Auctioneers

- *http://www.euroestates.pt/auctionlist.aspx?menuid=31*

- *http://www.uon-imobiliaria.pt/Imobiliario.aspx?lang=PT#/ mediacao/?vendidos=0&pagina=1&ordenacao=5*

Real estate agent

- *http://www.era.pt/campanhas/leiloes-de-casas_pt_1*

- *http://www.era.pt/vantagens/campanhas-showaspx?idcampanha= 1&title=leiloes-decasas&idcampanha=1&title=leiloes-de-casas& idioma=pt1*

Frequently, you can find real estate from banks for sale without auction. The sale is conducted by a real estate agent, who you should contact for detailed information about the property. The properties are listed as "Bank Properties".

A few examples:

Millennium BCP

- *http://ind.millenniumbcp.pt/en/Particulares/viver/Imoveis/Pages/ imoveis.aspx#/Search.aspx*

Caixa Geral de Depósitos

- *https://en.caixaimobiliario.com/buy-or-rent-in-portugal/real- estate-search-result.jsp?operacao=8*

Before going to an auction, you should make sure you visit the property. The portfolio of the properties at each auction lists the characteristics of every property and the contact details of the real estate agents responsible in setting up appointments for you to visit the property.

All auctions require you to sign in and pay a deposit, which is roughly between 5% and 10% of the reserve price. This deposit will be the down payment in case you make the winning bid. If you do not buy any property, at the end of the auction the deposit will be returned directly to you.

If you back out of the purchase after making the winning bid, you will lose your deposit.

Banks that are selling these properties may have specific financial solutions for particular properties at these auctions. This means the bank may be able to offer you a mortgage. Make sure you read the guidelines for the property or properties you are interested in. You should consult the regulations/conditions of each auction and make sure that you understand them.

Some of the banks in Portugal:

- Atlantico – Banco Portugues do Atlantico
- Banco de Portugal
- Banco 7
- Banco Portugues de Investimento (BPI)
- Banco Comercial Portugues
- Banco Espirito Santo
- Banco International de Credito S.A.
- Banco Mello
- Banco Santander Totta
- Banif – Banco Internacional do Funchal
- Banif Financial Group
- Barclays Netbanking Portugal
- BBVA Portugal
- Caixa Geral de Depositos
- Caixa Economica Montepio geral (CEMG)
- Cisf – Banco de Investimento S.A.
- Credito Agricola
- Espirito Santo Financial Group (ESFG)

STEP 6

CONTRACTS

Once you have chosen the property that you want and the seller has agreed on a price, you will then make a **"Contract of promise to buy and/or sell"**. This is only necessary in some situations if it is not possible to buy the property immediately.

If you can buy the property immediately, then you do not need contracts, lawyers, etc. You can set an appointment at the CASA PRONTA office. This is a government office where you can take care of **EVERYTHING** related to the purchase of the property at once.

Where can you find a CASA PRONTA office?

Updated list of offices:

*   *http://www.casapronta.pt/CasaPronta/conteudos/postos_ atendimento.jsp*

You can use any CASA PRONTA office, regardless of the region where your property is located. Just pick the office at your convenience or closest to where you are in Portugal.

If you are buying your property through a real estate agent, let the agent take care of this for you. It is a standard service for the agent to arrange this appointment and deliver the necessary paperwork to the CASA PRONTA office. This is a free service, no fees are charged by the real estate agent.

If you buy from a construction company, it is normal practice for the builder to take care of this appointment and paperwork; this is also free of any charges or fees.

If you are buying a property using a bank loan, the appointment can be made at the bank and the CASA PRONTA notary will go to the bank, if all members find it more convenient. In this case the appointment is scheduled online.

You do not have to do anything, since your bank credit manager will take care of it. This is also a free service.

All the documents the seller delivers to the CASA PRONTA office are going to be verified by the government office. These people are very professional and will detect if there is any legal problem with the property and inform you.

If you do not feel safe with the fact that your deed is going to be in Portuguese, ask for a copy of the draft a few days in advance and have it translated by someone you trust.

This deed is drafted by a government notary, not by the seller or anyone else.

Real estate agencies frequently provide translation services to the customer; the real estate agent will be present at the CASA PRONTA office to help you with any doubts you may have and to offer a translation service, especially when the customer is foreign. This is also free of charge.

Once you have an appointment set, you need to attend the appointment on time; some offices might cancel your appointment if you do not arrive at the scheduled time.

What you need to take:

- A bank issued cheque (money order) to pay for the property.
- Your ID
- Portuguese tax file number (see page 113 for details)
- A credit card, cash or check book to pay for the service fee and taxes.

- Your wife, husband or partner, if you are buying the property in joint names.

How much does it cost?

1. 700 € plus taxes: 2 registrations, i.e. registration of purchase and registration of a mortgage, if you use bank credit; or
2. 375 € plus taxes: 1 registration of purchase without the use of bank credit
3. The mentioned service fees.
4. The tax IMT: table in attachment (pp. 30-37)
5. The tax Imposto de Selo: 1%

Note: Some taxes may have small variations every year. This information is based on the 2014 tax rates

Portuguese: Tables de IMT 2014M Imposto Municipal Sobre As Transmissoes Onerosas de Imoveis

Continente

1. Aquisição de predio urbano ou fraccão autónoma de prédio urbano destinado exclusivamente à habitação própria e permanente:

CIMT – Art.° 17.° n.° 1-a)
Tabela Simplificada – Ano de 2014
Continente - Habitação própria e permanente

Rendimento Colectável (Euros)	Taxa Marginal a aplicar (em percentagem)	Parcela a abater (Euros)
Até 92.407,00	0%	0,00
De mais de 92.407,00 até 126.403,00	2%	1.848,14
De mais de 126.403,00 até 172.348,00	5%	5.640,23
De mais de 172.348,00 até 287.213,00	7%	9.087,19
De mais de 287.213,00 até 574.323,00	8%	11.959,32
Superior a 574.323,00	6%	0,00

2. Aquisição de predio urbano ou fraccão autónoma de prédio urbano destinado exclusivamente à habitação, não abrangido pelo quadro anterior:

CIMT – Art.° 17.° n.° 1-b)
Tabela Simplificada – Ano de 2014
Continente - Habitação

Rendimento Colectável (Euros)	Taxa Marginal a aplicar (em percentagem)	Parcela a abater (Euros)
Até 92.407.00	1%	0,00
De mais de 92.407,00 até 126.403,00	2%	924,07
De mais de 126.403,00 até 172.348,00	5%	4.716,16
De mais de 172.348,00 até 287.213,00	7%	8.163,12
De mais de 287.213,00 até 574.323,00	8%	11.035,25
Superior a 574.323,00	6%	0,00

Acquisição de prédios rústicos...5%

Acquisição de outros prédios urbanos e outras acquisições 6,5%

A taxa é sempre de 10%, nao se aplicando qualquer isenção ou redução sempre que o adquirente tenha a residência ou sede em país, território ou região sujeito a um regime fiscal mais favorável, constante de lista aprovada por portaria do Ministro das Finanças.

REGIÕES AUTÓNOMAS

1. Aquisição de prédio urbano ou fracção autónoma de prédio urbano destinado exclusivamente à habitação própria e permanente:

CIMT – Art.°17.° N.°1 – a] e Lei 2/90, de 4/8
Tabela simplificada – Ano de 2014
Regiões autónomas – Habitação própria e permanente

Rendimento Colectável (Euros)	Taxa Marginal a aplicar (em percentagem)	Parcela a abater (Euros)
Até 115.508,75	0%	0,00
De mais de 115.508,75 até 158.003,75	2%	2.310,18
De mais de 158.003,75 até 215.435,00	5%	7.050,29
De mais de 215.435,00 até 359.016,25	7%	11.358,99
De mais de 359.016,25 até 717.903,75	8%	14.949,15
Superior a 717.903,75	6%	0,00

2. Aquisição de prédio urbano ou fracção autónoma de prédio urbano destinado exclusivamente à habitação, não abrangido pelo quadro anterior:

CIMT – Art.°17.° N.°1 – a] e Lei 2/90, de 4/8
Tabela simplificada – Ano de 2014
Regiões autónomas – Habitação

Rendimento Colectável (Euros)	Taxa Marginal a aplicar (em percentagem)	Parcela a abater (Euros)
Até 115.508,75	0%	0,00
De mais de 115.508,75 até 158.003,75	2%	1.155,09
De mais de 158.003,75 até 215.435,00	5%	5.895,20
De mais de 215.435,00 até 359.016,25	7%	10.203,90
De mais de 359.016,25 até 717.903,75	8%	13.794,06
Superior a 717.903,75	6%	0,00

Tables de IMT 2014M Imposto Municipal Sobre As Transmissoes Onerosas de Imoveis – Translated in English
Tables of IMT 2014M The Municipal Tax on Property

Continent

1. Acquisition of urban building or autonomous fraction of urban building intended only for own habitation and permanent.

CIMT – Article.17, No.1-a
Simplified Table – Year 2014
Continent - Own permanent housing

Income Tax Rate Marginal Euros to be applied (in percentage)	Income Tax Rate Marginal Euros to be applied (in percentage)	Amount Deductable (Euros)
Up to 92.407.00	0%	0,00
Over 92.407,00 to 126.403,00	2%	1.848,14
Over 126.403,00 to 172.348,00	5%	5.640,23
Over 172.348,00 to 287.213,00	7%	9.087,19
Over 287.213,00 to 574.323,00	8%	11.959,32
Higher than 574.323,00 t	6%	0,00

2. Acquisition of urban building or autonomous fraction of urban building intended only for habitation, not included in the previous table.

CIMT – Article.17, No.1-b
Simplified Table – Year 2014
Continent – Housing

Income Tax Rate Marginal Euros to be applied (in percentage)	Income Tax Rate Marginal Euros to be applied (in percentage)	Amount Deductable (Euros)
Up to 92.407.00	1%	0,00
Over 92.407,00 to 126.403,00	2%	924,07
Over 126.403,00 to 172.348,00	5%	4.716,16
Over 172.348,00 to 287.213,00	7%	8.163,12
Over 287.213,00 to 574.323,00	8%	11.035,25
Higher than 574.323,00	6%	0,00

Acquisition of rustic building...5%

Acquisition of other urban buildings
and other costly acquisitions...6,5%

The rate is always 10%, not applying any exemption or reduction when the acquirer has the residence or registered office in country, territory or region subject to a more favourable tax regime, list of approved by order of the Minister of Financas.

AUTONOMAS REGIONS

1. Acquistion of urban building or autonomous fraction of urban building intended only for permanent residence:

CIMIT – Art.17, No.1 – a and law 2/90, of 4/8
Simplified Table Year 2014
Autonomas Region – Own habitation and permanent

Income Tax Rate Marginal Euros to be applied (in percentage)	Income Tax Rate Marginal Euros to be applied (in percentage)	Amount Deductable (Euros)
Up to 115.508,75	0%	0,00
Over 115.508,75 to 158.003,75	2%	2.310,18
Over 158.003,75 to 215.435,00	5%	7.050,29
Over 215.435,00 to 359.016,25	7%	11.358,99
Over 359.016,25 to 717.903,75	8%	14.949,15
Higher than 717.903,75	6%	0,00

2. Acquisition of urban building or autonomous fraction of urban building intended only for habitation not included in the above table:

CIMIT – Art.17, No.1 – b and law 2/90, of 4/8
Simplified Table Year 2014
Autonomas Region – Own habitation and permanent

Income Tax Rate Marginal Euros to be applied (in percentage)	Income Tax Rate Marginal Euros to be applied (in percentage)	Amount Deductable (Euros)
Up to 115.508,75	0%	0,00
Over 115.508,75 to 158.003,75	2%	1.155,09
Over 158.003,75 to 215.435,00	5%	5.895,20
Over 215.435,00 to 359.016,25	7%	10.203,90
Over 359.016,25 to 717.903,75	8%	13.794,06
Higher than 717.903,75	6%	0,00

I have attached a copy of the following contracts both in Portuguese and translated into English. These contracts are an example of what may be used when you purchase a property in Portugal. They are only meant to be used as a guideline as some contracts may vary.

1. A copy of a Housing Lease with an option to buy. Also known as a "Rent to Buy Contract".

2. Contracto De Compra E Venda – Urban Rent for Housing and Purchase Option Agreement.

3. Contracto De Permuta – Exchange Agreement (also known as a Swap).

4. Contracto de Promessa de Compra e Venda com reserve de Propriedade de Bens Movies – Purchase and Sale Agreement with Reserve Ownership of Personal Property.

You should also be aware that you can make a contract to your specific needs when purchasing a property; if the owner of the property agrees to the conditions outlined in your proposal, then that is your contract.

For example, going back to when I purchased my property, I offered three lump sum payments to be made over a six month period. The owner agreed to the terms in the proposal I made to purchase the property.

Portuguese: Casa Lease

Entre:..,
natural da freguesia e concelho ...., viúva,
titular do bilhete de identidade .... emitido em
.... pelos ...., contribuinte
fiscal no. ...., ...,
titular do bilhete de identidade no. .... emitido em
...., contribuinte fiscal no. ....
..................., ambas residentes na.............................., ...,
...., na qualidade de herdeiras ....
...., NIF de herança ....
..............., como PRIMEIRAS OUTORGANTES e SENHORIAS, e,
...., solteiro, maior, natural de
...., de nacionalidade alemã,
titular do passaporte no. ....
emitido em .... pela embaixada alemã em
Lisboa, contribuinte fiscal no. .... e ....
...., ..., natural
da freguesia de ...., concelho de ....,
titular do cartão de cidadão no. .... válido até
.... emitido pela República Portuguesa, contribuinte
fiscal no. ...., ambos residentes em ....
....,
como   SEGUNDOS   OUTORGANTES   e   INQUILINOS,   e
...., solteiro, maior,
natural de ...., Alemanha, de nacionalidade
alemã, titular do cartão de cidadão número ....
válido até .... emitido pela República Portuguesa,
contribuinte fiscal no. ...., residente em ....
.... Porches como
TERCEIRO OUTORGANTE E FIADOR é celebrado o presente

contrato de arrendamento habitacional nos termos do arto 1069 e seguintes do Código Civil, e que se rege pelas cláusulas seguintes:

Cláusula Primeira

As Primeiras Outorgantes são donas e legítimas proprietárias do prédio urbano destinado a habitação, sito em Rua do Sol também denominada ...., freguesia e concelho de ...., inscrito na respectiva matriz predial sob o artigo 741, descrito na Conservatória do Registo Predial de .... sob o no. ....

Parágrafo único: Prédio construído antes da data de ...., conforme certidão camarária de ....

Cláusula Segunda

Pelo presente contrato as Primeiras Outorgantes dão de arrenda-mento aos Segundos, o referido prédio, devoluto de pessoas e bens, pelo período de .... a ...., renovável automaticamente por períodos de 1 ano, se não fôr denunciado por qualquer das partes.

Parágrafo único – Em caso de venda do imóvel por parte das Primeiras Outorgantes, ficam os Segundos desde já, com direito de preferência nessa aquisição, acordando para esse efeito o valor de .... € , se decorridos 5 anos de arrendamento.

Cláusula Terceira

O preço acordado a pagar pelos Segundos Outorgantes às Primeiras foi determinado por ambas as partes da seguinte forma:

- Primeiro ano: 500,00 € (quinhentos euros) , mensais, pagos até ao dia 8 de cada mês, por transferência bancária para a conta ....
- Segundo ano: 550,00 € (quinhentos e cinquenta euros) mensais, pagos até ao dia 8 de cada mês, por transferência bancária para a conta ....
- Terceiro ano : 600,00 € (seiscentos euros) mensais, pagos até ao dia 8 de cada mês por transferência bancária para a conta ....
- Quarto e Quinto anos : 650,00 (seiscentos e cinquenta euros), mensais , pagos até ao dia 8 de cada mês por transferência bancária para a conta ....
- Com a assinatura do presente contrato os Segundos Outorgantes pagam a quantia de 1500,00 euros (mil e quinhentos euros).

Cláusula Quarta

- Os Segundos Outorgantes ficam desde já autorizados pelas Segundas Outorgantes a sublocar ou ceder no todo ou em parte, onerosa ou gratuitamente, o local arrendado.
- Os Segundos Outorgantes não podem realizar quaisquer obras que não sejam previamente autorizadas por escrito pelos Senhorios, e devidamente licenciadas que quando de beneficiação ou quando consideradas benfeitorias, ficam a fazer parte integrante do arrendado, sem direito a pagamento ou indemnização seja a que titulo ou natureza fôr.

Cláusula Quinta

Os inquilinos obrigam-se também, sob pena de indemnização a:

a) Com o termo do contrato abandonar o local deixando-o em bom estado de conservação como actualmente se encontra, funcionamento das instalações da rede de distribuição de água, electricidade, gás e esgotos, pagando à sua custa as reparações relativas a danificações.
b) Manter em bom estado as paredes, soalho e vidros.

Cláusula Sexta

O destino do arrendado é exclusivamente para habitação, não lhe podendo ser dado outro fim sob pena de resolução contratual.

Cláusula Sétima

O pagamento da água municipalizada, da energia eléctrica e saneamento básico, é da responsabilidade dos Segundos Outorgantes.

Cláusula Oitava

1. O Terceiro Outorgante, na qualidade de Fiador, procederá à respectiva renúncia do benefício de excussão prévia, assumindo de forma solidária, com os Segundos Outorgantes, o cumprimento estrito e pontual de todo o conteúdo versado no presente contrato de arrendamento.
2. Em conformidade com o no anterior, o fiador responderá ainda solidariamente por toda e qualquer alteração ou aditamento ao presente contrato.

3. No seguimento dos nos antecedentes, o seu conteúdo será válido, até à restituição do prédio objecto do presente contrato, livre quer de pessoas quer de bens.

4. Em tudo o que estiver omisso regulam as disposições legais aplicáveis.

_____

OS PRIMEIROS OUTORGANTES

O SEGUNDO OUTORGANTE

Casa Lease - English translation: Housing Lease

Between: _____,_____
parish of_____ and county of _____, (born
at _____), marital status _____, holder of
the identity document no _____ issued on _____ by
the Civil Identification Service of _____, taxpayer
identification no _____ and _____
parish of _____ and county of _____ (born
at _____), marital status _____, holder of
the identity document_____ issued on _____
by the Civil Identification Service of _____, taxpayer
identification number _____, both residents in
_____, as heirs of
_____, inheritance VATIN
no._____, as FIRST PARTIES and LORDSHIPS, and, __
_____, marital status
_____, of age, born in _____,
nationality _____, holder of the passport no _____
issued on _____ by the embassy _____ in _____,
taxpayer identification no _____
e _____, marital status_____,
parish of _____ , county of _____, holder of the
identity document no _____ valid until _____
issued by _____, taxpayer identification
no _____, both residents
in_____, as SECOND PARTIES and
TENANTS, and _____, marital status
_____, of age, born in _____, nationality
_____, holder of the identity document no _____
valid until _____ issued by _____,
taxpayer identification no _____, resident in
_____

as THIRD PARTIES AND SURETY, its celebrated the present housing lease in the terms article 1969 of the following of Civil Code and governed by the following clauses:

First Clause

The First Parties are the legit owners of the urban building for residential, in _____, parish of _____ and county of _____, written in the respective land register under the article no _____, described on the Land Registry of _____ under the no_____.

Single Paragraph: Building built before 7 August 1951, as certificate city council of _____

Second Clause

By the present contract the First Parties give housing lease to the Seconds, the said building, unoccupied by persons or goods, to the period of _____ to _____, automatically renewable for a period of 1 year, if not denounced by either party.

Single Paragraph - In case of sale of the immobile by the First Parties, the Seconds have the right of first refusal in that acquisition, having the for this effect the of _____, if elapsed 5 year lease.

Third Clause

The price settled to be paid by the Second Parties to the First was determined by both parties in the following way:

- First year: 500,00 € (five hundred euros) per month, paid until the 8th day of each month, by bank transfer to the account

  _____

- Second year: 550,00 € (five hundred and fifty euros) per month, paid until the 8th day of each month, by bank transfer to the account

  _____

- Third year: 600,00 € (six hundred euros) per month, paid until the 8th day of each month, by bank transfer to the account

  _____

- Fourth and Fifth Years: 650,00 (six hundred and fifty euros), per month, paid until the 8th day of each month, by bank transfer to the account

  _____

With the signature in the present contract the Second Parties pay the amount of _____ euros (_____ euros).

Fourth Clause

- The Second Parties become authorized by the First Parties to sublet or assign in whole or in part, costly or free, the leased site.
- The Second Parties can't make any works that are not previously authorized by the Landlords and properly licensed that when upgrading or when considered improvements, are an integral part of the leased, without right to payment or compensation to whatever title or nature is.

Fifth Clause

The tenants are forced to, under penalty of compensation:

a) With the term of contract abandoning the local, leaving it in good state as it is now, operation of the network facilities of water supply, electricity, gas and sewerage, paying at your cost the repairs relatively to the damage.

b) Maintain in good state the walls, floor and panes.

Sixth Clause

The destination is leased exclusively for housing and may not be given another order under penalty of contractual resolution.

Seventh Clause

The payment for the municipal water, electricity and sanitation is the responsibility of the Second Parties.

Eight Clause

1. The Third Grantor, as Surety, will proceed to renounce the benefit of prior prosecution, assuming solidarity with the Second Parties, the strict and punctual performance of all the content versed in this lease.
2. In accordance with the previous paragraph, the guarantor will also respond for any amendment or addendum to this contract.
3. Following paragraphs antecedents, its contents will be valid until the return of the building covered by this contract, free of people or goods.

In all that is missing regulate the legal provisions.

Place, _____

Date, _____

THE FIRST PARTIES

THE SECOND GRANTOR

Contrato de Arrendamento Urbano para fins Habitacionais e com Opção de Compra

Acrescentar ao contrato uma cláusula com o seguinte teor:

Cláusula Décima Segunda

O primeiro outorgante (senhorio) confere ao segundo outorgante (arrendatário) o direito de adquirir o imóvel objeto do presente contrato nos termos e condições constante do anexo 1 que dele faz parte integrante.

ANEXO 1

OPÇÃO DE COMPRA

1. O primeiro outorgante (senhorio) e o segundo outorgante (arrendatário) acordam que o preço de venda do imóvel objeto do presente contrato é de .... euros (por extenso).

2. Mais acordam que ao preço referido no número anterior serão deduzidas ....(percentagem) das rendas efetivamente pagas pelo segundo outorgante ao primeiro outorgante, no âmbito da vigência do contrato de arrendamento e que sejam devidas até à data do contrato de compra e venda.

3. O segundo outorgante poderá exercer o seu direito de opção de compra, nos termos referidos nos números anteriores, até cento e oitenta (180) dias antes da data do termo do contrato.

4. Caso o segundo outorgante não exerça o direito referido no número anterior, o contrato de arrendamento renovase por igual

período, sem prejuízo do direito de as partes se oporem à sua renovação, nos termos do disposto na lei.

5. Salvo acordo em contrário entre as partes, o não exercício do direito de opção de compra por parte do segundo outorgante, nos termos e condições referidos nos números anteriores, faz cessar o mesmo e, em consequência, fica sem efeito o disposto nos números um e dois deste anexo.

6. Sem prejuízo do disposto no número três, a opção de compra por parte do segundo outorgante poderá ser exercida a todo o tempo de vigência do presente contrato, mediante o envio de carta, por correio registado com aviso de receção, ao primeiro outorgante.

7. Caso o primeiro outorgante não cumpra com o acordado no presente anexo, não aceitando o exercício do direito de opção de compra nos termos definidos neste anexo e não comparecendo à celebração do contrato de compra e venda, é da sua responsabilidade devolver ao segundo outorgante a quantia de .... euros, correspondente a .... meses de renda, acrescida de juros de mora à taxa legal desde a data da comunicação do segundo outorgante até efetivo pagamento.

8. A marcação do contrato de compra e venda ficará a cargo do segundo outorgante, o qual deverá comunicar por escrito, em correio registado com aviso de receção, ao primeiro outorgante, o local, a data e a hora do referido contrato, com a antecedência mínima de oito dias da data agendada.

9. O imóvel objeto do presente contrato será vendido livre de quaisquer ónus e encargos.

10. São da responsabilidade do .... outorgante todas as despesas e encargos com a formalização do contrato devido pelo exercício do direito de opção de compra do imóvel

melhor descrito na cláusula....................., nomeadamente registos provisórios ou definitivos, Imposto Municipal sobre as Transmissões Onerosas (IMT), se a estes houver lugar, emolumentos notariais e toda a documentação

Feito em .... de .... de 2013, em duplicado, ficando um exemplar em poder de cada uma das partes.

Primeiro Outorgante

Segundo Outorgante

Urban Rent for Housing and Purchase Option Agreement

Add to the contract a clause which reads as follows:

Clause Twelve

The first party ……………………….……….………….….... (Landlord)
gives the second party …………………...…................... (Lessee)
the right to acquire the property …………………………………………
……………………………………………………………………………………

Object of this contract under the terms and conditions set out in Annex 1 which it is part.

ANNEX 1

OPTION

1. The   first   party   …………………………………………………
   (Landlord) and the second party……………………………………….
   (Lessee)   agree   that   the   selling   price   of
   ………………………………….………… Immovable object of
   this contract is ……………………………………………… Euros
   (Full amount).

2. Most agree that the price referred to above will be deducted
   …
   (Percentage) of income effectively paid by the second party to the first party within the term of the contract lease and that may be due up to the date of the purchase and sale agreement.

3. The second party may exercise its option to purchase under the terms set in earlier figures, one hundred and eighty (180) days before the date of expiry of the contract.

4. If the second party does not exercise the right referred to in the preceding paragraph, the lease renewal for the same period, without prejudice to the right of parties to oppose its renewal under provisions of the law.

5. Unless otherwise agreed between the parties, not to exercise of the purchase option by the second party, under the terms and conditions mentioned in the preceding paragraphs, stops the same, and therefore has no effect to the provisions of paragraphs one and two of this annex.

6. Without prejudice to paragraph three, the option to purchase by the second party can be exercised at any time of validity of this contract by sending a registered letter by mail with acknowledgment of receipt, to the first party.

7. If the first party fails to comply with the agreements in this Annex, not accepting to exercise the right to purchase option as defined in this annex and not attending the celebration purchase and sale agreement, it is your responsibility to give back to the second party the amount of ………………………………………………………… Euros, corresponding to ………………...................months' rent, plus interest at the legal rate from the date of communication of the second party until actual payment.

8. The marking of the purchase contract will be the responsibility of the second party, which shall by written notice, by registered post with acknowledgment of receipt, to the first party, the location, date and the time of the contract, at least eight days before the scheduled date.

9. The property subject of this contract will be sold free of all liens and charges.

10. Are the responsibility of the grantee ………….................. all expenses and charges related to the formalization of the contract due to the exercise of the option to purchase the best property described in clause ……………………………................., including temporary or permanent records, Municipal Tax Transmissions Costly (IMT), if there is such place, notary fees and all required documentation.

Made on …………………………..... of …………………………... 2013, in duplicate, and a copy held by each party.

First Party

Second Party

Contrato De Compra E Venda

PRIMEIRO

...

e

SEGUNDO

...

sobre a identificação das partes, vendedor e comprador, ver *"notas"* celebram entre si contrato de compra e venda, nos termos das cláusulas seguintes:

Primeira

Pelo preço de ... euros, que já recebeu e de que dá quitação, o PRIMEIRO vende ao SEGUNDO a fracção autónoma designada pela letra ..., correspondente a ..., do prédio urbano, sito em ..., freguesia de ... , concelho de ..., descrito na Conservatória do Registo Predial de ... sob o número ... da freguesia de ..., submetido ao regime da propriedade horizontal nos termos da inscrição F - ..., inscrito na matriz predial urbana sob o artigo ..., sendo de ... euros o valor patrimonial da fracção autónoma, que está registada a favor do vendedor pela inscrição G- ....

Segunda

A fracção autónoma é vendida livre de ónus ou encargos, ficando assegurado o cancelamento da hipoteca registada a favor de ... pela inscrição C - ....

Terceira

Para o prédio/para a fracção autónoma ora transmitida   foi   emitido pela Câmara Municipal de …, no dia …,   o alvará de autorização de utilização no….   /O prédio foi inscrito na matriz em data anterior a 1951,   não sendo exigível   licença de utilização.

Quarta

O SEGUNDO aceita a venda, destinando a fracção adquirida a habitação própria permanente.

1. *O SEGUNDO aceita a venda, destinando a fracção adquirida a habitação própria permanente.*

2. *O Comprador utilizou no pagamento, a quantia de …   euros, proveniente de conta "Poupança-Habitação", titulada em seu nome, e aberta há mais de um ano, junto do Banco ….*

Quinta

A ficha técnica do imóvel será entregue pelo PRIMEIRO   ao SEGUNDO no acto de autenticação do presente contrato.

Sexta

…   não exerceu o respectivo direito legal de preferência.

Sétima

No presente negócio interveio   F ...,   mediador imobiliário/ sociedade de mediação imobiliária, titular da   licença no.   ... / registado(a) no Instituto da Construção e do Imobiliário, I.P., sob o no. .... /As partes não recorreram a mediação imobiliária.

local: _____

data: _____

assinaturas: _____

TERMO DE AUTENTICAÇÃO

No dia ... , em ....[i], perante mim, ... [ii], compareceram:

> *sobre a identificação das partes [vendedor e comprador], demais intervenientes e sobre a verificação da respectiva identidade, ver notas"*

que, para autenticação, me apresentaram o contrato de compra e venda anexo, declarando que já o leram/que estão perfeitamente inteirados do seu conteúdo, que exprime a sua vontade [e/ou a vontade do seu Representado].

E que, advertidos de que, nos termos do disposto no artigo 40.o da Lei n.o 15/2013, de 8 de fevereiro, o cliente de empresa de mediação imobiliária que omita a informação sobre a intervenção desta no contrato incorre na pena aplicável ao crime de desobediência previsto no art.o 348.o do Código Penal, declararam ainda que, para a compra e venda, recorreram a mediação imobiliária prestada por ..., titular da licença n.o ... /registado(a) no Instituto da Construção e do Imobiliário, I.P. sob o no. ... / não recorreram a mediação imobiliária.

Verifiquei:

* a identidade das partes ... e a qualidade e poderes para o presente acto ... [iii];

* sobre a verificação da identidade das partes e demais intervenientes, ver notas"

- os elementos registrais da fracção autónoma transmitida por consulta da certidão permanente de registo predial, com o código de acesso n.o ... /por certidão do teor da descrição e das inscrições em vigor, emitida pela Conservatória ... , no dia ..., que exibiram;

- os elementos matriciais por consulta da caderneta predial ... /por caderneta predial/certidão do teor da inscrição matricial/ comprovativo da declaração para inscrição ou actualização da inscrição de prédios urbanos na matriz (modelo 1) emitido no dia ... , que exibiram;

Exibiram:

- alvará de autorização de utilização n.o ..., emitido para a fracção autónoma/para o prédio[iv] pela Câmara Municipal de ..., no dia/ certidão de escritura pública, da qual consta que para o prédio/para a fracção autónoma vendida[v], foi emitido pela Câmara Municipal de ..., no dia ... , o alvará de autorização de utilização n. o ... /caderneta predial emitida no dia ..., da qual consta que o imóvel foi inscrito na matriz em data anterior a 7 de Agosto 1951/certidão emitida pela ... no dia ..., comprovativa de que o prédio foi edificado antes de 7 de Agosto de 1951, pelo que a respectiva utilização não estava sujeita a licenciamento municipal];

- a ficha técnica da habitação[vi], neste acto entregue ao comprador

Ficam arquivados:

- documento único de cobrança do imposto municipal sobre as transmissões onerosas de imóveis n.o ... , no valor de ... , liquidado no dia … e pago no dia, e o extracto da declaração para a liquidação [vii];

* documento único de cobrança n.o …   , comprovativo do pagamento do imposto do selo da verba 1.1 da tabela geral, no valor de …, liquidado no dia … e pago no dia … , e o extracto da declaração para a liquidação.

* declaração emitida pelo Banco …   no dia, comprovativa de que o comprador utilizou na aquisição do imóvel o montante de …,   proveniente da conta poupança-habitação que tem naquela instituição bancária, tendo respeitado o prazo contratual mínimo de um ano de imobilização [viii].

As partes foram advertidas da anulabilidade/ ineficácia do acto em relação a … por … [ix].

O presente termo de autenticação foi lido e explicado, em voz alta e na presença simultânea de todos os intervenientes

[assinaturas das partes, demais intervenientes[x] e da entidade autenticadora]

Contrato De Compra E Venda – Translated in English

Contract of Purchase and Sale

PURCHASE AND SALE AGREEMENT

FIRST

....

And

SECOND

....

On the identification of the parties, seller and buyer.

Celebrate each other a contract of sale, pursuant to the following clauses:

First

For the price of .... euros, which has already received and giving discharge, the FIRST .... and SECOND.. sells the building unit designated by the letter .... corresponding to ...., the urban building located in ...., parish ...., municipality ...., described in the Land Registry under number .... of

…………………………………….. the ……………………….... parish, submitted to the horizontal property regime under the F inscription - …………………………………….., registered in the urban land register under article ……………………………………., being EUR ……………………………………. the book value of the building unit which is registered to the seller by the G-registration……………………....

Second

The building unit is sold free of liens or encumbrances, being assured the cancellation of the registered mortgage in favor of the C ……………………….... description - ………………………………....

Third

For the building / building unit for now transmitted was issued by the city of …, on …, the use permit authorizing No …………….. /………..… The building was entered in the matrix on a date prior to 1951, not being required license to use.

Fourth

THE SECOND accepts the sale, allocating the fraction acquired permanent residence.

1. *THE SECOND accepts the sale, allocating the fraction acquired permanent residence.*

2. *The Purchaser used to pay the sum of … euros, from "housing savings" account, titled in his name, and open more than a year, with the Bank ….*

Fifth

The Property sheet will be delivered by the SECOND FIRST in the authentication act of this contract.

Sixth

.... Did not have the lawful right of first refusal.

Seventh

In this business intervened F ..., real estate agent / company real estate, holder of license No ... / registered (a) at the Institute of Construction and Real Estate, IP, under paragraph .... / The parties did not use the Realtor.

Location: _____

Date: _____

Signatures: _____

TERMS OF AUTHENTICATION

On ....………….   on   ………….............,
Before me, …........……………, attended: ……………………………

On the identification of the parties [seller and buyer], other stakeholders and the verification of their identity.

That, for authentication, showed me the contract of sale attached declaring to have read / who are perfectly acquainted of its content, expressing his will [and / or the will of his Represented].

And that, advised to pursuant to Article 40 of Law No 15/2013 of 8 February, the real estate company client that omit information about its involvement in the contract incurs the penalty applicable to the crime of disobedience provided for in article 348 of the Penal Code also stated that, for the purchase and sale, resorted to real estate provided by ..., holder of license No ... / registered (a) at the Institute of construction and Real Estate, IP under the No ... / did not use the Realtor.

Checked:

• The identity of the parties ... and the quality and power to the act …………………………………...; on the identity of the parties and other stakeholders.

• Register the elements of the building unit transmitted by consulting the permanent certificate of land register, with no access code …………………………………………….…... / …………… certificate by the description of the content and registrations in force, issued by the Registry ..., on ..., which exhibited;

- The matrix elements by consulting the property book
  ………………………………………………….. / by building book
  / content of the certificate of registration matrix / statement
  attesting to registration or update registration of urban property
  in the matrix (model 1) issued on the day …………………….....
  which exhibited;

Exhibited:

- No use of authorization permit ... issued for the building unit / to
  the building by the city of ..., on / certificate of a public deed, which
  states that for the building / building unit sold for, was issued by
  the City Council of ... on ... the use permit authorizing n. No ... /
  land passbook issued on ..., which states that the property was
  entered in the matrix on a date prior to August 7, 1951 / certificate
  issued by ... on ... to prove that the building was built before 7
  August 1951, so their use was not subject to municipal licensing];

- The data sheet housing, hereby delivered to the buyer

Are filed:

- Single document the collection of municipal tax on
  onerous transfer of property No……………………….. worth
  ……………………………………………………………….., settled on
  …………………………………………….... and paid on the day,
  and the declaration of the extract to the settlement;

- Single document collection …………………………………
  …
  No, proof of payment of the amount of stamp duty 1.1
  of the general table, worth…………………………………,
  settled on ……………………………………….. and on

…………………………..... paid, and the declaration statement for settlement.

- Statement issued by the Bank ... on the day, stating that the buyer used the property purchase the amount of ……………………………… ……………………………………… from the savings account housing that has that bank, have complied with the minimum contract period of one year of detention.

The parties were advised of nullity / ineffectiveness of the act from the ……………………………………………. by ……………………………… ……………………………………….………………………………………………

This authentication term was read and explained, loudly and in the simultaneous presence of all stakeholders

…………………………….   …………………………..…..

Name……………………….   **Name**…………………….…..

[Signatures of the parties, other stakeholders and the authenticating entity]

CONTRATO DE PERMUTA

PRIMEIRO

...

e

SEGUNDO

...

sobre a identificação das partes, ver "*notas*"

celebram entre si contrato de permuta, nos termos das cláusulas seguintes:

Primeira

Que são donos e legítimos possuidores:

- o PRIMEIRO da fracção autónoma designada pela letra ... , correspondente a ... , destinada a ... , do prédio urbano, sito em ... , na freguesia de ... , concelho de ... , descrito na Conservatória do Registo Predial de ... sob o número ... da freguesia de ... , submetido ao regime de propriedade horizontal nos termos da inscrição F - ... , registada a seu favor pela inscrição G - ... , inscrito na matriz predial urbana sob o artigo ... , com o valor patrimonial de ... euros, a que atribuem o valor de ... euros, e será designada IMÓVEL UM.

- o SEGUNDO de ... , a que atribuem o valor de ... euros, e será designado IMÓVEL DOIS.

Segunda

Sobre o IMÓVEL UM incide uma hipoteca a favor de … , para garantia de empréstimo concedido ao PRIMEIRO, registada pela apresentação … , cujo cancelamento está assegurado.

O IMÓVEL DOIS está livre de qualquer ónus ou encargo.

Terceira

Pelos valores acima atribuídos, o PRIMEIRO cede o IMÓVEL UM ao SEGUNDO, que em troca lhe dá o IMÓVEL DOIS e … euros, em dinheiro, importância de que dá quitação.

Quarta

1. Para o prédio de que faz parte o IMÓVEL UM foi emitida em … , pela Câmara Municipal de … , a autorização de utilização no … .

2. Para o IMÓVEL DOIS foi emitida em … pela Câmara Municipal de … , autorização de utilização no … .

Quinta

As fichas técnicas dos imóveis permutadas serão entregues no acto de autenticação deste contrato.

Sexta
(Mediação imobiliária)

No presente negócio interveio F … , mediador imobiliário/sociedade de mediação imobiliária, titular da licença n.o … /registado(a) no Instituto da Construção e do Imobiliário, I.P., sob o n.o … . /As partes não recorreram a mediação imobiliária.

Sétima

As Partes destinam os imóveis que acabam de adquirir a habitação própria permanente.

Local: _____

Data: _____

Assinaturas: _____

TERMO DE AUTENTICAÇÃO

No dia … , em ….[xi], perante mim, … [xii], compareceram:

sobre a identificação das partes, demais intervenientes e sobre a verificação da respectiva identidade, ver *"notas"*

que, para autenticação, me apresentaram o contrato de permuta anexo, declarando que já o leram/que estão perfeitamente inteirados do seu conteúdo, que exprime a sua vontade [e/ou a vontade do seu Representado].

E que, advertidos de, que nos termos do disposto no artigo 40.o da Lei n.o 15/2013, de 8 de fevereiro, o cliente de empresa de mediação imobiliária que omita a informação sobre a intervenção desta no contrato incorre na pena aplicável ao crime de desobediência previsto no art.o 348.o do Código Penal, declararam ainda que, para a permuta, recorreram a mediação imobiliária prestada por … , titular da licença n.o … /registado(a) no Instituto da Construção e do Imobiliário, I.P. sob o n.o … / não recorreram a mediação imobiliária.

Verifiquei:

- a identidade das partes … e a qualidade e poderes para o presente acto … [xiii];

- sobre a verificação da identidade das partes e demais intervenientes, ver "notas"

- os elementos registrais de … por consulta da certidão permanente de registo predial, com o código de acesso n.o …

/por certidão do teor da descrição e das inscrições em vigor, emitida pela Conservatória … , no dia …, que exibiram;

os elementos matriciais de … por consulta da caderneta predial … /por caderneta predial/certidão do teor da inscrição matricial/ comprovativo da declaração para inscrição ou actualização da inscrição de prédios urbanos na matriz (modelo 1) emitido no dia … , que exibiram;

Exibiram:

• alvará de autorização de utilização n.o …, emitido para a fracção autónoma/para o prédio[xiv] pela Câmara Municipal de …, no dia/ certidão de escritura pública, da qual consta que para o prédio/para a fracção autónoma permutada[xv], foi emitido pela Câmara Municipal de …, no dia … , o alvará de autorização de utilização n. o … /caderneta predial emitida no dia …, da qual consta que o imóvel foi inscrito na matriz em data anterior a 7 de Agosto 1951/certidão emitida pela … no dia …, comprovativa de que o prédio foi edificado antes de 7 de Agosto de 1951, pelo que a respectiva utilização não estava sujeita a licenciamento municipal;

• a ficha técnica da habitação[xvi], neste acto entregue a … .

Ficam arquivados:

• documento único de cobrança do imposto municipal sobre as transmissões onerosas de imóveis n.o … , no valor de … , liquidado no dia … e pago no dia, e o extracto da declaração para a liquidação [xvii];

• documento único de cobrança n.o … , comprovativo do pagamento do imposto do selo da verba 1.1 da tabela geral, no valor de …, liquidado no dia … e pago no dia … , e o extracto da declaração para a liquidação.

As partes foram advertidas da anulabilidade/ ineficácia do acto em relação a … por … [xviii].

O presente termo de autenticação foi lido e explicado, em voz alta e na presença simultânea de todos os intervenientes

[assinaturas das partes, demais intervenientes[xix] e da entidade autenticadora]

Contrato De Permuta – Translated in English

EXCHANGE AGREEMENT

FIRST

....

And

SECOND

....

On the identification of the parties,

Celebrate each other exchange agreement, pursuant to the following clauses:

First

Who are owners and rightful owners:

- The FIRST of the condominium unit designated by the letter ...., corresponding to ...., destined to, the urban building located in .... in the parish of .... county ...., described in the Land Registry under number .... of .... the parish of .... submitted to the horizontal property regime under the registration F -

…………………………………….., recorded in his favor by the inscription G - ………………………..... inscribed in the urban land register under the article …………….. with a book value of ……………………………………….. euros, which assign the value ………………………………….. of euros, and will be designated a PROPERTY.

- The SECOND of ………………………………………….. the value of that attribute ……………………………….. euros, and will be assigned TWO PROPERTY.

Second

PROPERTY ONE focuses on a mortgage in favor of

…………………..……………. for loan guarantee granted to FIRST, registered by the presentation …………………………………. whose cancellation is assured.

TWO STILL is free from any burden or charge.

Third

The values assigned above, the FIRST cedes the SECOND ONE PROPERTY, which in turn gives you ……………………………. and STILL TWO euros in cash importance of giving discharge.

Fourth

1. For a building that is part of the BUILDING ONE …………………………………………….... was issued by the Municipality of…………………………………………….....authorization to use …………………………………………….. no.

2. For TWO STILL was issued by the city of ……………………… ……………………………….……………………… authorization …………………………………….... no use.

Five

Data sheets exchanged properties will be handed in the act of authentication of this contract.

Sixth

(Real estate agencies)

In this business intervened F ……………………………………..., Real Estate Agent / Realtor Company, holder of License No. ……………………………………. / Registered (a) at the Institute of Construction and Property, IP, under no …………..... /

The parties have not resorted to Realtor.

Seventh

Parties are designed for homeowners who end up purchasing their own permanent housing.

Location: _____

Date: _____

Signatures: _____

TERMS OF AUTHENTICATION

On ………………………………….. of ……………...………………….. ,
Before me, ……………......... attended: …………………………………..

On the identification of the parties, and other stakeholders on the verification of their identity, that for authentication, showed me the exchange agreement attached, stating that since the read / who …………………………………………………………………………are perfectly acquainted their content, which expressed its desire [and / or the will of his Represented].

And who advised that pursuant to Article 40 of Law No. 15/2013, of February 8, the client real estate company that omits information about its involvement in the contract incurs a penalty applicable to the crime of disobedience envisaged in article 348 of the Penal Code also stated that, for exchange, turned to real estate …………………………………….... provided by, the holder of license No …………………………….... / registered (a) at the Institute of Construction and Property, IP under the No …………………………………….... / not resorted to Realtor.

Checked:

- The identity of the parties ……….……………………......……… and the quality and powers for the act...………………………….……;

Checking the identity of the parties and other participants.

- Registered the elements ……….…………………………… by consulting the permanent certificate of land registration, with no access code ……….……………………….. / certificate for the content of the description and registrations in force issued by the Registrar ……………….….. in the day …………………………………………. that exhibited;

- The matrix elements of the building ……………………….. for consultation ……………………………….. book / passbook for building / contents of the certificate matrix / registration statement for proof of enrollment or updating of registration of urban properties in the matrix (model 1) issued on …………….. that exhibited;

Exhibited:

- No permit authorizing use ………………………………………………… issued to independent / fraction to the building by the City Council of …………………………………………………. on / certificate deed, which states that for the building / condominium unit exchanged for, was issued by the City Council of …………………………….. on ………………………………………. the permit authorizing use n. No ………………………….. / land passbook issued on …………………….., which states that the property was inscribed on the array placed before August 7, 1951 / certificate issued by ………………….. on …………….. stating that the building was built before 7 August 1951, so that their use was not subject to local licensing;

- Datasheet housing, hereby given to …………………………..

Are filed:

- Single document collection of municipal tax on onerous transfer of property ………………………………………….. No, worth ………………………….. liquidated ……………………….. and paid on the day, and the extract of the declaration for the settlement;

- No single document collection ……………………….., proof of payment of stamp budget of 1.1 overall tax table, worth ………………………….. liquidated ………………….. and paid on the day …………………….. and the extract of the declaration for the settlement.

The parties were advised of annulment / nullity of the act in relation to .... by ....

This term authentication was read and explained, aloud and in the simultaneous presence of all stakeholders

[Signatures of the parties, other stakeholders and the authenticating entity]

CONTRATO DE PROMESSA DE COMPRA E VENDA

ENTRE:

.... (nome), natural de ...., contribuinte fiscal no. ....
e .... natural de ...., contribuinte fiscal no. ....,
casados no regime de comunhão de adquiridos, residentes em
......................., ambos como **Vendedores**;

E

.... (nome), solteiro, maior, natural de ...., contribuinte no
.............., residente na ...., adiante designado por **Comprador**,

**É mutuamente acordado e aceite o presente contrato de compra
e venda, nos termos e cláusulas seguintes:**

Cláusula 1.ª

Os **Vendedores** são proprietários de um conjunto de máquinas
destinadas à indústria de restauração, devidamente descritas e
identificadas na lista anexa ao presente contrato, dele fazendo parte
integrante.

Cláusula 2.ª

Pelo presente contrato, os **Vendedores** vendem ao **Comprador**,
que por sua vez lhes compra, livres de quaisquer ónus, encargos ou
responsabilidades, as referidas máquinas de restauração.

Cláusula 3.ª

1. O preço da compra e venda é de €. .... (......... de euros), pagos da seguinte forma:

   a) €. .... (........de euros) na data da celebração do presente contrato;

   b) €....... (....de euros), ou seja, a parte restante, deverá ser paga em prestações mensais de €: ....(......de euros), durante os próximos doze meses, ou seja de ..... a .... inclusive.

Cláusula 4.ª

A presente venda é feita com reserva de propriedade para os vendedores até que o preço se encontre integralmente pago, não obstante as referidas máquinas terem sido entregues na presente data ao **Comprador**.

Cláusula 5.ª

As prestações mensais referidas na cláusula 3.ª b) deverão ser entregues até ao quinto dia útil de cada mês na residência dos **Vendedores**.

Cláusula 6.ª

1. As partes desde já acordam que o **Comprador** entrará de imediato em mora se se atrasar no pagamento de qualquer uma das prestações dentro do prazo acima estabelecido, devendo, neste caso, entregar a prestação em falta acrescida de mais 50% até ao vencimento da próxima prestação.

2. Se se encontrarem em falta prestações que excedam 1/8 do preço total, os **Vendedores** deverão estabelecer um limite

máximo para o cumprimento das mesmas, acrescidos dos 50% acima referidos, informando o **Comprador** por carta registada com aviso de recepção desse novo prazo.

3. Se após o vencimento do novo prazo estabelecido o **Comprador** continuar em falta, o presente considera-se automaticamente resolvido.

4. Caso se verifique a situação prevista no número anterior, o **Comprador** deverá devolver, no prazo máximo de 48 horas, todas as máquinas objecto do presente contrato, sendo responsável pela sua entrega na residência dos **Vendedores** em perfeito estado de conservação.

O presente contrato rege-se, em tudo o que for omisso, pela lei portuguesa, nomeadamente por todas as disposições do Código Civil e demais legislação aplicável.

Feito e assinado em Lisboa, em ..... de .... de......, em dois exemplares iguais, entregues a cada uma das Partes.

Os Vendedores

_____

O Comprador

_____

Contrato de Promessa de Compra e Venda – Translated in English
Purchase and Sale Agreement with Reserve
Ownership of Personal Property

BETWEEN:

....
(Name), natural .... and no taxpayer ....
....natural, no
taxpayer .... married in the regime of community
acquired residing in ...., both as sellers;

And

.... (Name),
single, largest, natural ....
No taxpayer resident in ....
.........., Hereinafter referred to as

Buyer,

It is mutually agreed and accepted this contract of sale, the following terms and provisions:

Clause 1

Sellers are the owners of a set of machines for the catering industry, properly described and identified in the list attached to this contract, made part.

Clause 2

By this agreement, the Vendors sell to Buyer, which in turn purchase them, free of any liens, charges or liabilities, such machines restoration.

Clause 3

1. The purchase price and sales is €…………………..................
   ………. (………………………………………………….. Euro), payable as follows:

   a) €………………………………........ (………………….in Euros)
      on the date of execution of this contract;

   b) € ……………………………........ (…………………………
      de Euros), ie, the remainder shall be paid in monthly
      instalments   of   €:………………………………………
      (………………….......... EUR) during the next twelve
      months,   ie   …………………………………….   including
      the…………………………………………………………………..

Clause 4

This sale is made subject to reservation of ownership to the sellers until the price lies fully paid, despite these machines have been delivered to Buyer on the date hereof.

Clause 5

The monthly instalments referred to in clause 3 b) must be delivered by the fifth working day of each month at the residence of the Sellers.

Clause 6

1. The Parties hereby agree that the Purchaser will immediately be in default if delay in payment of any instalment payment within the period specified above, and in this case delivering the benefit in increased another 50% to the lack of maturity next instalment.

2. If there are missing benefits that exceed 1/8 of the total price, the Sellers shall establish a maximum limit for the fulfilment of the same, plus the 50% above, informing the Purchaser by registered letter with acknowledgment of this new term.

3. If after the expiry of the new deadline Buyer continues to default, this is considered to be automatically solved.

4. If the situation provided for in the preceding paragraph, Buyer shall return, within 48 hours, all machines covered by this contract and is responsible for its delivery at the residence of the Sellers in perfect condition.

This contract shall be governed in all that is silent, under Portuguese law, in particular by the provisions of the Civil Code and other applicable law.

Done and signed at .... on the .... of .... in two identical copies, delivered to each party.

Sellers

_____

The Buyer

_____

CASA SIMPLES CASA SEGURA

casasimples
casa**segura**

Perguntas & Respostas

1. O que é a "Casa Simples - Casa Segura"?

A "Casa Segura" consiste num **atendimento personalizado e altamente qualificado**, sem balcões, com boas instalações e adequada tecnologia de ponta, onde é possível realizar todas as operações relativas a contratos, nomeadamente à compra e venda de casa, com ou sem empréstimo, num único local: o cartório notarial.

O seu notário, que é um **jurista, profissional imparcial e com qualificação de excelência, está sempre presente na celebração de contratos, que são redigidos um a um, à medida dos seus interesses; o notário protege todas as partes envolvidas.**

Este procedimento "Casa Segura" foi desenvolvido pela Ordem dos Notários tendo em vista a **prestação de serviços cada vez mais eficientes aos cidadãos e às empresas.**

Consulte o sítio *http://www.notarios.pt*

Na "Casa Segura" é possível:

a)   obter **conselho jurídico** desde o início da contratação (contrato-promessa), **imparcial** e em defesa de todos os intervenientes no negócio,

b)   obter a caderneta predial gratuita,

c)   obter uma certidão predial permanente gratuita,

d)   obter uma certidão comercial permanente,

e)   obter certidões do registo civil (de óbito, de casamento e de nascimento),

f)   obter, em geral, todos os documentos necessários à formalização do contrato,

g)   celebrar contratos,

h)   realizar imediatamente todos os registos, com um desconto de 20% (via on line),

i)   **pagar impostos e cumprir obrigações fiscais,** nomeadamente:

   1 - o imposto do selo e o IMT,
      (e, com a sua senha das declarações electrónicas:)
   2 - pedir a isenção de pagamento do Imposto Municipal sobre Imóveis (IMI),
   3 - pedir a alteração da morada fiscal,
   4 - apresentar a declaração Modelo 1 do IMI (inscrição ou a actualização de prédio urbano na matriz),
   5 - apresentar a Modelo 1 do imposto de selo (IS) - relação de bens.

2.   Onde funciona a Casa Segura?

Na **rede** de cartórios notariais, a **única com cobertura a nível nacional.**

3.   Posso utilizar a Casa Segura para qualquer imóvel ou sociedade, em qualquer ponto do País?

Sim.

4. Para que tipo de negócios posso utilizar a Casa Segura?

Para todos (prédios, empresas e automóveis), nomeadamente:

a) Contratos-promessa;

b) Compra e venda, com ou sem empréstimo;

c) Divisões de coisa comum e permutas;

d) Empréstimos bancários e respectivas transferências;

e) Hipotecas;

f) Locações financeiras e respectivas cessões de posição contratual;

g) Testamentos, habilitações e partilhas por óbito e por divórcio;

h) Repúdios e renúncias de herança;

i) Constituições e renúncias ao direito de usufruto;

j) Doações;

k) Justificações;

l) Constituições e alterações de propriedade horizontal;

m) Constituições de direitos reais, como servidões ou direito de superfície;

n) Registo predial on line, com 20% de desconto;

o) Convenções antenupciais;

p) Arrendamentos, trespasses e locações de estabelecimentos comerciais e industriais;

q) Contratos de trabalho;

r) Constituições de sociedades de todos os tipos;

s) Alterações de pacto social, aumentos e reduções de capital;

t) Cessões de quotas e acções;

u) Fusões e cisões de sociedades;

v) Dissoluções e liquidações de sociedades;

w) Constituições de associações e fundações e respectivas alterações.

x) Registo comercial on line, com 50% de desconto;

y) Registo automóvel on line, com 50% de desconto.

5. Para que outro tipo de situações posso utilizar a Casa Segura?

a) **Para me certificar de que o vendedor tem todos os documentos em ordem;** o mediador imobiliário ou o técnico oficial de contas podem indicar-me um notário a quem recorrer antes de pagar qualquer sinal.

b) Para **ver certificados quaisquer factos que o notário presencie, os quais fazem prova plena de certos acontecimentos, até em tribunal; um certificado pode fazer a diferença, pode evitar um processo judicial ou torná-lo mais rápido.**

Exemplos:

- certificado dos bens que compõem o recheio de uma casa em determinada data,
- o que ficou depois de um assalto,
- o conteúdo de um cofre,
- o estado de uma obra,
- que uma casa tem humidades,
- que mudaram a fechadura da sua porta.

c) Para **tratar de um caso transfronteiriço.**

Exemplos:

- habilitação de uma pessoa de nacionalidade francesa, com aplicação da lei francesa,
- partilha de bens de um cidadão russo que deixou bens em Portugal e em Espanha,
- alteração dos estatutos de uma sociedade italiana,
- cessão de uma quota de uma sociedade alemã,
- procuração para um belga vender bens localizados Malta.

Os notários de Portugal fazem parte da Rede Notarial Europeia (RNE), composta por um delegado sediado em cada um dos países da UE. Visite o sítio:

http://www.cnue-nouvelles.be/en/reseau-notarial-europeen-en/001/index.html

O delegado da RNE em Portugal é a notária

Professora Doutora Ana Luísa Balmori Padesca
Ordem dos Notários
Travessa da Trindade, 16-2oC
1200-469 Lisboa
Tel : +351-213468176
Fax : +351-213468178
E-mail : internacional@notarios.pt

A referida delgada portuguesa da RNE podem ser consultada por qualquer cidadão, entidade ou empresa sobre a lei portuguesa ou leis europeias; neste último caso, a delegada contacta com o delegado do país europeu em causa e transmite a informação assim obtida a quem a solicitou.

Só o documento feito por notário (autêntico) circula livremente em todos os países da EU.

6. Posso utilizar a Casa Segura para qualquer imóvel, independentemente da sua localização territorial?

Sim. O notário pode celebrar escrituras de quaisquer imóveis ou empresas, aqueles localizados, independentemente da localização do imóvel ou da sede da empresa.

7. Posso utilizar a Casa Segura se pedir um financiamento ao banco para a compra de casa? E se não pedir?

Posso utilizar em ambas as situações.

8. Quanto custa utilizar a Casa Segura? É mais barato que seguir o procedimento "normal"?

O notário é retribuído nos termos de tabela aprovada pelo Ministério da Justiça.

Os honorários do notário são calculados com base no custo efectivo do serviço prestado, tendo em consideração a natureza dos actos e a sua complexidade.

O notário deve proceder com moderação, tendo em vista, designadamente, o tempo gasto, a dificuldade do assunto, a importância do serviço prestado e o contexto sócioeconómico dos interessados.

O acompanhamento da contratação pelo notário permite que o utente escolha o caminho fiscalmente mais favorável, uma redução de custos com os registos predial, comercial e automóvel e poupar no processo de obtenção de documentos.

Nos custos finais, a Casa Segura é a única que lhe permite verdadeiramente poupar quantias avultadas, pelo que é muito mais barata do que a Casa Pronta das conservatórias ou qualquer outro balcão único.

9. Que vantagens tenho em utilizar a Casa Segura?

a.) A Casa Segura é um procedimento realizado através de um notário, jurista altamente especializado, que presta conselho jurídico desde o início do processo, nomeadamente em colaboração com a instituição de crédito que intervenha no contrato, e aponta o caminho mais favorável ao utente, naquele caso concreto, nomeadamente em matéria fiscal.

b.) O notário é um profissional imparcial, que protege todas as partes envolvidas num negócio; só o notário é que faz escrituras: se o seu notário assinou, o seu contrato está garantido.

c.) Todas as operações se fazem num único local, o cartório, evitando-se deslocações, filas, senhas e esperas; o sistema informático também é seguro e de capacidade adequada aos respectivos fins.

    i) A Casa Segura permite fazer num único momento o contrato e o respectivo registo.

    ii) O notário pode liquidar o imposto sobre as transmissões onerosas de imóveis (IMT), o imposto do selo (IS), e, a solicitação do utente e com a respectiva senha das declarações electrónicas, que o notário também pode solicitar, o notário pode ainda pedir a isenção de pagamento do Imposto Municipal sobre Imóveis (IMI), a alteração da morada fiscal, pode apresentar relações de bens (heranças – Modelo 1 do IS) e ainda a declaração Modelo 1 do IMI (inscrição ou a actualização de prédio urbano na matriz).

    iii) Nesta última situação, não se torna necessário solicitar as plantas do imóvel à câmara municipal, porque é o notário que o faz e as envia ao serviço de finanças.

d.) É um processo simplificado, com menos formalidades; deixa de ser necessário ir à conservatória, porque o negócio jurídico é celebrado perante o notário, que imediatamente procede à realização do registo. Deixa, ainda, de ser necessário:

    i) Obter junto da conservatória do registo predial uma certidão do prédio antes de celebrar uma escritura pública, porque o notário requisita no início do processo uma certidão predial on line, permanentemente actualizada;

ii) Obter na conservatória do registo comercial, uma certidão de registo comercial- quando o interveniente seja uma pessoa colectiva -, porque o notário tem acesso à base de dados do registo comercial, em tempo real, com o código da respectiva certidão permanente;

iii) Obter na conservatória do registo civil certidões de óbito, casamento ou nascimento, porque o notário trata desse assunto directamente;

iv) Obter na repartição de finanças a caderneta predial, porque o notário tem acesso à base de dados das cadernetas prediais;

v) Obter na câmara municipal uma certidão da licença de habitação, porque o notário trata desse assunto directamente.

e.)   O preço é mais barato.
O notário é retribuído nos termos de tabela aprovada pelo Ministério da Justiça.

Os honorários do notário são calculados com base no custo efectivo do serviço prestado, tendo em consideração a natureza dos actos e a sua complexidade.

O notário deve proceder com moderação, tendo em vista, designadamente, o tempo gasto, a dificuldade do assunto, a importância do serviço prestado e o contexto sócioeconómico dos interessados.

O acompanhamento da contratação pelo notário permite que o utente escolha o caminho fiscalmente mais favorável, uma redução de custos com os registos predial, comercial e automóvel e poupar no processo de obtenção de documentos.

Nos custos finais, a Casa Segura é a única que lhe permite verdadeiramente poupar quantias avultadas, pelo que é muito mais barata do que a Casa Pronta das conservatórias ou qualquer outro balcão único.

f) Posso **proceder logo ao cumprimento de obrigações fiscais,** após a aquisição de um imóvel: apresentar o pedido de isenção do IMI, apresentar a declaração Modelo 1 do IMI (inscrição ou a actualização de prédio urbano na matriz), e apresentar o pedido de alteração da morada fiscal.

g) **Posso proceder logo ao cumprimento de obrigações fiscais**, após a habilitação de herdeiros: apresentar a Modelo 1 do imposto de selo (IS) - relação de bens.

10. Posso marcar um dia para ir ao notário celebrar o contrato?

Sim. Pode telefonar ou enviar um email para os contactos que constam em *http://www.notarios.pt/OrdemNotarios/PT/PesquisaNotarios/* ou marcar pessoalmente **junto de um qualquer cartório mais próximo de si. O banco que tratar do financiamento também pode fazer a marcação prévia por via electrónica.**

Também é possível utilizar a **Casa Segura sem realizar qualquer marcação prévia,** mas, mesmo nesse caso, não é imposto um modelo de contrato pré-aprovado.

11. O notário também trata do direito de preferência?

Sim. O vendedor deixa de ter de se relacionar com várias entidades públicas diferentes (por ex. o IGESPAR, I.P., municípios, etc.) para transmitir a informação necessária ao exercício do direito de preferência por várias vias diferentes e formas diferentes. **Basta contactar o notário.**

12. Na Casa Segura estou dispensado de ir ao IGESPAR, I.P. e/ou à câmara para saber se querem exercer o direito de preferência?

Sim. Estes actos passam a ser tratados pelo notário. Depois tem que esperar 10 dias úteis, que é o prazo que as entidades com direito legal de preferência têm para manifestar a intenção de exercer esse direito.

13. Que documentos devo levar para celebrar contratos na Casa Segura?

Os documentos de identificação e os cartões de contribuintes dos vendedores e dos Compradores, os respectivos regimes de bens, se casados, e as moradas. Sempre que o prédio tenha ficha técnica, é preciso levá-la.

Se tiver uma escritura pública de uma transacção anterior do mesmo imóvel onde esteja referida a existência de licença de utilização, ou a sua dispensa, devo levá-la.

Se, no meu caso, forem necessários outros documentos, serei informado disso pelo notário, pessoalmente, por email ou pelo telefone.

14. Preciso de ir à câmara municipal para obter uma certidão da licença de habitação e levá-la para a compra e venda na Casa Segura?

Não. O notário trata disso por si.

15. Tenho de pagar o IMT nas finanças antes de fazer a compra e venda através da Casa Segura?

Não. Pode ser feito no cartório.

16. Tenho de pagar antes nas finanças o imposto de selo para poder utilizar a Casa Segura?

Não. Pode ser feito no cartório.

17. Quando se celebra o contrato na Casa Segura quanto tempo demora a realização dos registos?

É imediata. Assinado o contrato, não tenho que me deslocar novamente à conservatoria para pedir os registos. **O notário requisita-os on line, com 20% de desconto.**

18. Se quiser mudar a minha morada fiscal para a nova casa que acabei de comprar na Casa Segura tenho de ir às finanças?

Não. Posso fazê-lo na Casa Segura.

19. Se quiser pedir dispensa de pagamento de IMI depois de comprar uma casa na Casa Segura tenho de ir às finanças?

Não. Posso fazê-lo no cartório.

20. Depois de comprar uma casa na Casa Segura tenho de ir à câmara recolher as plantas (telas finais) da casa para as entregar nas finanças?

Não. O notário assegura a recolha dessas plantas e o seu envio para as finanças. O interessado deixa em qualquer caso de ser onerado com essa obrigação.

21. Depois de comprar uma casa na Casa Segura tenho de ir às finanças pedir uma caderneta actualizada em meu nome?

Não. Logo que disponível na base de dados, o notário recolhe-a e envia-a gratuitamente por correio ou para o seu email.

22. Só a Casa Segura me dá segurança?

Sim. Nos sistemas que recorrem à contratação sem recurso a notário **um quarto das transacções resultam de falsas declarações,**

de hipotecas falsas e de bens inexistentes (de acordo com as estatísticas do FBI, de Janeiro de 2009).

É este o sistema que o actual executivo quer adoptar em Portugal. Será que o quer para si?

**SÓ SE O SEU NOTÁRIO ASSINOU
É QUE O SEU DIREITO ESTÁ GARANTIDO.**

Casa Simples Casa Segura – Simple Home, Safe Home - Translated in English

casasimples
casa**segura**

Questions & Answers

1. What is "Casa Simples - Casa Segura"?

"Casa Segura" consists in a highly qualified and personalized service, without restrictions, with good facilities and proper cutting-edge technology where it is possible to perform all operations about contracts namely the purchase and selling of houses with or without a loan, in a single spot: the public notary.

Its notary, a professional and impartial jurist with excellent qualification, will present the contracts, that are written by one tailored to your interests: the notary protects all the parties involved.

This procedure "Casa Segura" was developed by the Civil Law Notary aiming for better services for citizens and companies.

Consult the website *http://www.notarios.pt*

With "Casa Segura" it's possible to:

a)   receive impartial legal advice since the beginning of the contract (promise contract) defending all the parties involved in the business,

b)   receive for free the Legal Description, receive for free a permanent property registry certificate, receive a permanent commercial certificate, obtain a civil registration certificate (death, marriage and birth), obtain, in general, all the necessary documents for the contract formalization, celebrate contracts, perform immediately all the registrations, with 20% of discount (online) pay taxes, fulfill fiscal obligations, namely:

- stamp duty and property tax,
  (with password of the electronic statements)
- ask for payment exemption of Property Tax,
- ask for alteration of tax address,
- show the declaration of Model 1 of Property Tax (subscription or update of urban building in matrix),
- present Model 1 of stamp duty - the goods

2. Where does "Casa Segura" operate?

It operates in Civil-Law Notaries, the only one with national coverage.

3. Can I use "Casa Segura" in any office or society anywhere in the country?

Yes.

4. For what kind of business can I use "Casa Segura"

For all (buildings, companies, cars), namely:

a)   Promise contracts;
b)   Purchase and Sale, with or without loan;
c)   Division and exchange of common things;
d)   Bank loans and transfers;
e)   Mortgages;
f)   Finance leases and respective assignments of their contractual position;
g)   Wills, qualifications and shares by death and marriage;
h)   Renunciation of inheritances;

i)   Constitutions and waivers to the right of uses;
j)   Donations;
k)   Justifications;
l)   Constitutions and alteration of horizontal property;
m) Constitutions of real rights as easements and surface;
n)   Land register online with 20% off;
o)   Prenuptial agreements;
p)   Rents, goodwills, leases of commercial and industrial establishments;
q)   Work contract;
r)   Society constitutions of all kinds;
s)   Change of social pact, capital increases and decreases;
t)   Concession of quotas and stocks;
u)   Mergers and corporate divisions;
v)   Dissolution and liquidation of companies;
w) Associations and foundations constitutions and amendments;
x)   Commercial register online with 50% off;
y)   Automobile register online with 50% off.

5. For what type of situations can I use "Casa Segura"?

To make sure that the seller has all documents in order; the real estate agent or registered auditor can indicate a notary to ensure that everything is in order before paying.

To see the certificates of any facts the notary witness, that are proofs of certain events, until reaches the court; a certificate can make the difference, avoid a lawsuit or make it faster.

Examples:

The goods certificate that compose The household effects, what remained after an assault, the content of a safe, the state of a work, that a house has humidities, that the lock house was changed.

c)   To treat a border case.

Examples:

Qualifications of a person with French nationality with application of the French law, share of goods of a Russian citizen that left goods in Portugal and in Spain, statute change of an Italian society, cession of a quota of German society, proxy for a Belgian to sell goods located in Malta.

 The notaries of Portugal are part of the Europe Notaire, composed by a delegate hosted in each country of EU. Visit the website: *http://www. cnue-nouvelles.be/en/reseau-notarial-europeen-en/001/index.html*

The delegate of the Europe Notaire in Portugal is the notary:

Doctor Professor Ana Luísa Balmori Padesca
Civil-Law Notary
Travessa da Trindade, 16-2oC
1200-469 Lisbon
Tel : +351-213468176
Fax : +351-213468178
E-mail : internacional@notarios.pt

The mentioned Portuguese delegate of Europe Notaire can be approached by every citizen, entity or company under the Portuguese law or European laws; in this case the delegate contacts the delegate of the European country concerned and transmits the obtained information of the person who requested.

Just the authentic document made by the notary will freely circulate in all EU countries.

6. Can I use the "Casa Segura" to any office, independently of its localization?

Yes. The notary can finalize legalities for any real estate or companies, independently of the localization of the office and the companies' headquarters.

7. Can I use "Casa Segura" if I ask for a bank loan in order to buy the house? And if not?

I can utilize it in both situations.

8. How much it costs to use "Casa Segura"? Is it cheaper than the normal proceeding?

The notary is rewarded in the chart terms approved by the Justice Ministry.

The notary's fees are calculated based on the cost of the provided service considering the nature of the acts and their complexity.

The notary must proceed with moderation having in mind the time spent, the difficulty of the subject, the importance of the subject and the socioeconomic context of stake holders.

The monitoring of the hiring by the notary permits the person to choose the fiscal path more favorable, costs reductions with the land, automobile and commercial registry this way saving in the process of obtaining the documents.

In the final costs, "Casa Segura" is the only one that permits you to save a considerable amount, cheaper than the "Casa Pronta" of register or any other fees.

9. What advantages do I have using "Casa Segura"?

"Casa Segura" is a procedure realized through a notary, a highly specialized jurist that provides law advice since the beginning of the process namely in collaboration with the credit institution that intervenes in the contract and points the easiest way to the person in that specific case, speaking about fiscal matter.

The notary is an impartial professional that protects all parties involved in the business; only the notary makes the scriptures: if your notary signed, your contract is guaranteed.

All the operations are made on a single spot- the registry- this way avoiding dislocations, queues, passwords and waitings; the informatic system is safe and with enough capacity for the respective purposes.

The "Casa Segura" permits making in a single moment the contract and respective register.

The notary can liquidate the property taxes, the stamp duty, and the wearer solicitation with the respective password of the electronic declarations that the notary can also request the notary can even ask payment exemption of Municipal Property Taxes, change the tax address, present the relationships goods (inheritances - Model 1 of stamp duty) and even the declaration Model 1 of Municipal Property taxes (subscription or update of the urban building of the matrix).

In the last situation, it's not necessary request the plants property in the city council because the notary is the one who does it and sends them to the Finanças.

It's simple process with less formalities; it's not necessary to go to the registry because the legal business is celebrated in front of the notary that immediately precedes the register.

It's no longer necessary:

Obtain in the Land Registry the building certificate before celebrating a public scripture because the notary requests in the beginning of the process an updated building certificate online;

Obtain in the Commercial Registry a commercial certificate - when the intervening is a collective person - because the notary has access to the database of the permanent commercial registry in real time with the respective code.

Obtain in the registry of Vital Records death, marriage or birth certificates because the notary treats that matter directly.

Obtain in the Income Tax Department the building book because the notary has access to the database of building books;

Obtain in the City Council a certificate of housing license because the notary takes care of that matter directly.

The price is cheaper.

The notary is rewarded in the chart terms approved by the Justice Ministry.

The notary's fees are calculated based on the cost of the provided service considering the nature of the acts and their complexity.

The notary must proceed with moderation having in mind the time spent, the difficulty of the subject, and the importance of the subject and the socioeconomic context of stakeholders.

The monitoring of the hiring by the notary permits the wearer choose the fiscal path more favorable, costs reductions with the land, automobile and commercial registry this way saving in the process of obtaining the documents.

In the final costs, "Casa Segura" is the only one that permits you to save considerable amounts which is cheaper than the "Casa Pronta" of register or any other areas.

I can proceed right away with the fulfilment of fiscal obligations after the acquisition of a immobile: submit the application to exemption the Municipality Property Taxes, present the declaration Model 1 of Municipal Property Taxes (subscription or update of the urban building of the matrix) and show the request to change the tax address.

I can proceed right away with the fulfilment of fiscal obligations after the qualification of heirs: show Model 1 of stamp duty - relationships goods.

10. Can I make an appointment any day to go to the notary celebrate the contract?

Yes. You can call or send an e-mail for the contracts that included on *http://www.notarios.pt/OrdemNotarios/PT/PesquisaNotarios/* or make a personnal appointment in the nearest Register Office. The bank that will take care of the loan can also make an appointment electronically. It is also possible use "Casa Segura" without making a previous appointment but in that casa it's not imposed a pre-approved contract.

11. The notary also takes care of the rights of first refusal?

Yes. The seller has no need to connect with various public entities (municipalities, IGESPAR, etc.) to transmit the necessary information to practise the rights of first refusal through many ways and forms. Just contact the notary.

12. In "Casa Segura" am I relieved of going to IGESPAR, I.P and/or city council to know if they want to fulfil the rights of first refusal?

Yes. These acts can be taken care of by the notary. Then you have a deadline of 10 days to manifest the legal right of preference.

13. What documents do I have to take to celebrate the "Casa Segura" contracts?

The identification documents, cards of taxpayers, sellers and buyers, their schemes of goods, if married, and addresses. If the building has datasheet, you need to take it.

If you have a deed from a previous transaction of the same property where is mentioned the existence of a license, or his discharge, you need to take it. If, in your case, other documents are required, you will be informed of this by the notary in person, by email or phone.

14. Do I need to go to the City Council to obtain a certificate a housing license and take to purchase and sell in "Casa Segura"?

No. The notary takes care of that for you.

15. Do I have to pay Municipal Property Taxes in finances before purchasing and selling through "Casa Segura"?

No. It can not be done in the office.

16. Do I have to pay before in the Finances the stamp duty to use "Casa Segura"?

No. It can be done in the Register Office.

17. When the contract is signed in "Casa Segura" how much time it takes the registers?

It's immediate. When the contract is signed, you dont' need to return again to the registry to ask for the registers. The notary requests them online, with 20% off.

18. If I want to change my tax address to the new house I just bought in "Casa Segura" do I have to go to the Finances?

No. You can do it in "Casa Segura".

19. If I want to ask for exemption of payment of Municipal Property Taxes after buying the house in "Casa Segura" do I have to go to the Finances?

No. You can do it in the Register Office.

20. After buying a house with "Casa Segura" do I have to go to the City Council collect the houseplans to deliver it to the Finances?

No. The notary makes sure to collect those houseplans and its sending to the Finances. The interested is not obligated concerning that issue.

21. After buying a house with "Casa Segura" do I have to go the Finances ask for updated booklet in my name?

No. As soon it is available in the database, the notary collects it and sends if for free by post or to your e-mail.

22. Only "Casa Segura" gives me safety?

Yes. The systems that resort to hiring without a notary, a quarter of the transactions end up in false declarations, false mortgages and non-existent goods (according to the FBI statistics, January 2009)

IF YOUR NOTARY SIGNED THEN YOUR RIGHT IS GUARANTEED.

STEP 7

LEGAL REPRESENTATION

When you have decided you wish to make an offer on a property, prior to submitting that offer, ensure that you find a lawyer (in Portuguese it is an Advogado for a male and an Advogada for a female).

For legal representation in Portugal, it is best to use an advogado if you are not fully aware of the processes, don't speak Portuguese or you do not have anyone to represent you in Portugal. In Australia, America and the UK, this is equal to the services of a solicitor, lawyer or barrister.

An advogado is legally accountable for all the advice they give to you regarding the purchasing of a property and all their actions pertaining to the purchase of your property.

The advogado fees are regulated by the **Ordem dos Advogados** and you can research further through them if necessary.

Your advogado will instruct and assist you in agreeing to the terms of a contract when purchasing a property, and can structure a contract to the buyer's terms. You can make a contract in regards to a singular payment or multiple payment structures, without the aid or use of a bank.

For example, at the time of purchasing my Figueira da Foz property I did not have the full amount in cash on the offer that I made to the owner. My advogado was able to structure my contract so that I paid three separate payments; the first two payments being 20,000 € each and the third payment was 25,000 €, paid over a six month period.

During that six month period, I was able to obtain the money a lot quicker than expected and was able to settle within three months instead of six months.

I did not use a bank at all to acquire my property and also, for your information, no bank in Australia (that I was able to find at the time) would lend me money to buy a property overseas.

Referring back to my contract, as I had to return home to Australia for work before the contract was signed, I signed "Power of Attorney" documents for my advogado to act on my behalf, so the advogado signed for me, once the owner had signed the papers agreeing to my offer.

As the owner at the time was living in Luxemberg, it took a while for her to complete the signing of the contracts as she also had to sign for someone else in Portugal to act on her behalf; in this case it was the owner of the real estate agency that I had bought the property through.

Website and Directory Addresses for all Adgovados in Portugal;

https://www.oa.pt/CD/Servicos/PesqAdvogados/pesquisa_adv. aspx?sidc=31634&idc=5&idsc=31897

STEP 8

FISCAL NUMBER

Tax File Number

Most Portuguese will already have a registered Fiscal Number; foreigners or non-residents will need to obtain one.

A Fiscal Number (also known as a **Numero Fiscal de Contribuinte**) is obtained from the local tax office. I found it was easier to apply for mine at the local office in the area where I bought my property.

The Figueira da Foz office was very obliging in helping me to obtain a Fiscal Number; I also had the help and guidance of my advogado, and at the time it cost me nothing.

Your Fiscal Number is used on all documents relating to the purchase of a property and the paying of rates to the local council (also known as the **Camara** in Portuguese).

If you are purchasing a property as partners (two or more) or a married couple, each person needs to obtain an individual Fiscal Number or the tax department will not accept the transfer tax, rates or stamp duty on the property.

You cannot obtain a Fiscal number online; you should go in person to the office to do this, as they need to physically check your identification. However, this can be done by your representative, such as your advogado, who will, in turn, be responsible for the information given to the Financas.

The documents you need to produce to apply for a Fiscal number will be any photo identification, such as a driver's licence, passport or national identity card.

Once you have provided these, you will be issued with a printout of your fiscal number. You can then register online at:

https://www.portaldasfinancas.gov.pt/pt/home.action

Within a couple of days you will receive a password so that you can check your taxes online. A card with your Fiscal number on it should be posted out to you within 7-14 days. You can use your advogado's postal address for this if you do not have a residential address in Portugal.

For any other information you may require or are interested in, you can go online to the following Financas web address which explains the Portuguese tax system in English:

http://info.portaldasfinancas.gov.pt/pt/docs/Conteudos_1pagina/ NEWS_Portuguese_Tax_System.htm

In Portugal, foreigners may be advised that they need a Fiscal representative to obtain a Fiscal Number, for a fee of an estimated 250 €. This is not true; there are no fees or charges applied in obtaining a Fiscal Number.

Your advogado or real estate agent can assist you with this. You will need to supply, if a foreigner, your home country tax file number **(documented from your country of residence; for example, your tax return for the last three years and your payslips, where your tax file number is listed, for the last three months).**

Numero de Identificacao Fiscal –
Pessoa Singular – Ficha de Inscricao

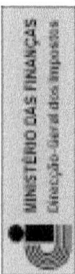

Application for Tax File Identification Number, Single Person Registration Form – Translated in English to corresponding numbers

1. Name
2. Resident
3. Residence Number
   1. Street
   2. Number
   3. Floor
   4. Locality
   5. County
   6. Parish
   7. Post Code
   8. Parents
   9. Region/Territory
   10. Telephone
   11. Email
4. Birthplace
   1. County
   2. Parish
   3. Parents

5. Nationality
   1. Portuguese
   2. Other
6. Date of Birth
7. Sex
   1. Female
   2. Male
8. Documents of Identification
   1. Ticket of Identification
   2. Birth Certificate
   3. Passport
   4. Other
9. Identification of Representative
   1. Fiscal Number
   2. Name
   3. Signature of Representative
10. Financas Service Officers details and signature

Where Original is that is for both the applicant and the Identification of Representation (your representative) to declare that everything stated is true and correct and for both persons to sign the declaration.

Instrucoes Para o Preenchimento

O preenchimento da presente ficha destina-se à inscrição, para atribuiçâo do número de identificaçâo fiscal de pessoa singular, a que se encontrarn obrigadas nomeadamente todas as pessoas singulares com rendimentos sujeitos a imposto. ainda que dele isentos.

- Preencher esta ficha de acordo com os dados constantes do DOCUMENTO DE IDENTIFICAÇÃO (BILHETE DE IDENTIDADE, CÉDULA PESSOAL, PASSAPORTE OU OUTRO) E USANDO LETRAS MAIÚSCULAS (A, B, C, ... Z).

- Para os residentes todos os campos, excepto 3.9, 3.10, 3.11 e quadro 9, são de preenchimento obrigatório.

- Pode ser entregue em qualquer Serviço de Finanças ou Serviço de Apoio ao Contribuinte.

QUADRO 3 - Como domicilio fiscal entende-se o local da residência habitual (n° 1 do art° 19° da L.G.T). Tratando-se de não residente deve ser indicada a morada no país da residência. considerando-se, todavia domiciliado na residéncia do representante.

No campo 3.9 deve ser ainda mencionada a região ou território, se constar da lista aprovada pela Portaria no. 1272/2001, de 9 de Novembro.

QUADRO 4 - Se nasceu no estrangeiro. indique somente o país. Se nasceu em Portugal preencha apenas o concelho e freguesia.

QUADRO 9   - Este quadro destina-se a designar, nos termos do art.° 130° do CIRS, urna pessoa singular ou colectiva com residência em Portugal para o representar perante a Direcção-Geral dos Impostos.

NOTE BEM - O DUPLICADO desta ficha fica em poder do contribuinte que o utilizará como prova da sua entrega.

- A gestão do processamento de dados compete à Direcção de Serviços de Cadastro da DGCI - Apartado 8143- 1802 -001 LISBOA

- Todos os dados destinam-se a recolha informática, com excepção dos averbados no quadro 8 (Documento de Identificação)

Instrucoes Para o Preenchimento –
Instructions for filling an application for a
Tax Identification Number - Translated in English

The Tax Identification Number (NIF) is the tax identification number of individual taxpayers in Portugal, assigned by the General Director of Taxes and Contributions.

It is a card that identifies the citizen taxpayer before the tax administration.

Citizens can purchase the application form for the card through the Portal of Finance or in offices of DGCI Citizen offices.

The application is free and the NIF will be assigned immediately upon presentation of proof of identification.

Any Portuguese citizen, Community member or foreign national may require the NIF, who are residing or working in Portugal.

If you are not a resident you must appoint a tax representative. You need to request the document at DGCI, taking with you a valid ID (Passport or Document of Civil Identification) and fill out the appropriate forms.

The NIF may also be required by a tax representative by submitting a power of attorney document for this purpose and an identity document, duly authenticated by the party represented.

After the documents have been submitted and the identification verified you will be given a NIF and the NIF card will be delivered with confirmation of the registration to the address given or to the nominated person whom you have given power of attorney to.

STEP 9

POWER OF ATTORNEY

The legal responsibilities to your property
that your advogado will ensure are fulfilled.

If you are Portuguese and are working or travelling overseas for longer than 3 months, please ensure that you give Power of Attorney over your property to an advogado or to someone you can trust, to ensure that all legal obligations are fulfilled whilst you are not in the country.

If you are a foreigner who is not residing in Portugal you will have to ensure that you give your advogado Power of Attorney for your property.

This basically means he/she will ensure that all your legal responsibilities to your property are fulfilled. For example, your advogado will contact you requesting that you send money to pay for your rates to the Camara, your water and electricity bills, etc.

Your advogado will look after anything relating to your property and inform you of all your obligations to the property, which he will assist you in fulfilling.

Make sure that you outline the responsibilities you expect your advogado to fulfil. Do not give them all the powers (e.g. to sell your property, unless you are selling it), only the power to act on your behalf regarding the maintenance costs of your property (e.g. water, electricity, gas, rates and insurance).

The same applies if you have a friend or family member acting on your behalf in your absence, concerning the responsibilities of your property.

An alternative to this is to set up a direct debit system with your bank to pay all the financial responsibilities for your property automatically; therefore, you don't need to rely on anyone, except maybe for someone to pass by and check to see if your property is ok whilst you are not in Portugal.

STEP 10

NOTARY

Third Party involved binding both parties
to the contract of sale terms and conditions.

This is where both the seller and buyer agree to a contract of sale and the Notary is a third party who signs the contract that binds the first two parties to the agreement.

The fees are an estimated 30 € to sign the contract.

To register the contract it costs approximately 289 €.

List of some documents needed to buy or sell a property in Portugal:

1. Seller and buyer ID or passport (individuals)
2. Commercial Certificate, representative ID, Pact of the Society (companies)
3. Fiscal Number (Tax file number, see page 113)
4. Power of Attorney and ID of the procurator in case of use of a procurator (a procurator is a person, deputy or agent who manages the affairs of another)
5. Actual Land Carnet or Certificate of the Article content
6. Certificate content descriptions and registrations in effect (or code to access)
7. License of use in case of urban property, or certificate proving that your presentation is dispensed because it was built before August 7, 1951
8. Demonstrating guide payment of Stamp Tax Transmissions and Municipal Tax (IMT)
9. Technical description of the property (buildings after 2004)
10. Energy certificate (This will be provided to you by the real estate agent or seller of the property)

 # (1) At the time of writing this book, all information is true and correct.

STEP 11

LIENS & MORTGAGES
ON THE PROPERTY

Your advogado will check the property for any liens or mortgages (first and second mortgages against the property) so that there are no outstanding legal restraints on the property.

Alternatively, you can do it yourself through the departments as listed in the Government Auction in Step 4; refer to page 15.

For example; my Figueria da Foz property had one (1) lien, a first mortgage and a second mortgage on the property; the interest rates on the outstanding monies the owner had against the property were eating away any profit she might have made on it.

As it was, once my advogado had paid the mortgages and the lien (apparently the owner owed the real estate agent 5,000 € or thereabouts) the owner only ended up receiving around 5,000 €.

This was pretty sad in any event; most of the money from the sale of the property had to repay interest and back payments, as she was behind on her loan repayments.

My advogado made sure all the money I had paid went directly to the mortgages and the lien, before giving the rest to the real estate agent and the former owner.

They also ensured that no other loans were given against my property before it was deeded into my name, registering me as the legitimate owner.

STEP 12

FOREIGN CURRENCY EXCHANGE

How to send your money
overseas to another country.

Transferring any amount of money overseas can be quite daunting for most people. When I bought my property in Portugal, I did an international transfer through my Australian bank, thinking that it was the best method. I have since learnt that this is not the case.

I lost thousands of dollars by using my Australian bank to transfer money overseas at the bank's conversion rate AUD (Australian dollars) to Euros.

Since then, I have researched a number of ways to get the best value I possibly could in converting AUD to Euros.

The best I found for myself was the Foreign Currency Exchange (FC Exchange). It cost me a $20.00 AUD fee from my bank to send my money in Australian dollars to the FC Exchange, where they in turn would convert to Euros.

The FC Exchange then converted my currency at a much better rate than my bank would have given me. At times, I have saved at least $500 AUD by using FC Exchange as opposed to my bank.

The first time I transferred my money through the FC Exchange I was so worried they were going to steal my money and I would never see it again. Now I laugh to myself every time I send money.

The FC Exchange charges $15 AUD to convert the money and send it to your nominated bank account. It normally takes between 3 and 5 days to transfer the money to the FC Exchange in the United Kingdom (UK) and for them to then transfer the money to the bank account I have nominated. Normally, once the FC Exchange has received my money, they transfer it out on the same day.

In the last 12-18 months I've transferred nearly $100,000 AUD to Portugal and I have never had a problem with the FC Exchange.

Information about the Foreign Currency Exchange Company;

Address: FC Exchange | 10th Floor | 88 Wood Street | London | EC2V 7RS

Contact Numbers:

T: +44 (0)20 7989 0000
Fax : +44 (0)20 7989 9999

Website: *www.fcexchange.co.uk*

FC Exchange is a trading name of Foreign Currency Exchange Limited.

Foreign Currency Exchange Limited is a limited company registered in England and Wales.

Registered office: 88 Wood Street, 10th Floor, London, EC2V 7RS.

Registered number: 5452483.

Foreign Currency Exchange Limited is authorised by the Financial Services Authority (No. 511266) under the Payment Service Regulations 2009 for the provision of payment services.

H M Customs & Excise MLR No.12215508.

Please note that Foreign Currency Exchange Limited may monitor email traffic data and also the content of email for the purposes of security and staff training.

What you will need to forward to FC Exchange to register as a client;

- Payslips – Copies of the last 10 payslips
- Bank Statements – For the last 3 months
- Passport – Copy of
- Driver's Licence – Copy of

Once the Foreign Currency has received all this information you will then be sent an email that looks something like this;

* * *

Dear Miss/Mrs/Mr_____,

I am pleased to confirm your Trading Account with Foreign Currency Exchange has been **opened**. In order to **activate** your account, money laundering regulations dictate we must receive photographic identification (e.g. a copy of passport photo page or photo ID driver's license) and proof of physical address (e.g. utility bill –*excluding internet bills*, or a bank statement that is no more than 3 months old). Please either post your documentation or scan and email it to *info@fcexchange.co.uk*

It is my pleasure to welcome you as a client by confirming your account reference details:

Client Reference Code:

Your FCE Broker:

Foreign Currency Exchange are passionate about providing clients with competitive pricing and our team of dedicated brokers will take the time to understand your currency requirements.

You are now eligible to purchase your currency. Remember your broker cannot secure a rate of exchange without your instruction. Once this has been received a contract confirming the trade will be issued to you immediately via email, fax or post. It is important to remember that your currency is purchased in a live market, cannot be altered or cancelled and must be settled in accordance with the relevant contract conditions.

You will be required to settle trades by transferring funds to the Foreign Currency Exchange Client Account, details of which can be found on the contract and below. You can also transfer funds prior to executing a trade and execute when you choose. Always attach your unique client reference when transferring funds to Foreign Currency Exchange as this allows us to quickly identify your monies. Please also let us know if you choose to settle from a bank account other than one in your name as this allows us to deal with your transfer swiftly and avoid delays.

Account Name:	**FC Exchange AUD Client Account**	Please provide your bank with the following special instruction:
Bank:	**Barclays Bank**	**"Do Not Convert Currency"**
Branch:	**93 Baker Street London W1A 4SD**	
Account no:	**GB46 BARC 2006 0558 0373 33**	This can be included in the reference or special instruction field of the payment
Swift:	**BARCGB22**	
Reference:	**Your client Reference no.**	

*Please note the account details provided are specifically for **AUD** payments to us, if you require alternative currency account details to make a payment please contact us on **0800 783 4313** or **+44 (0) 207 989 0000**. The amount indicated on the confirmation is the amount Foreign Currency Exchange will have sent. Some banks may levy a small receiving or routing charge and should this happen then please address it with your bank and use our confirmation as proof of entire fund remittance.*

Yours Sincerely,
Head of Compliance

FCExchange | 10thFloor | 88WoodStreet | London | EC2V 7RS
T: +44 (0)20 7989 0000 | F: +44 (0)20 7989 9999

* * *

Once you have received this, you can then send money to your FC Exchange account. Please make sure you send money in Australian dollars or your country's currency.

When the money has been received by FC Exchange, they will then send you an email, confirming that they have received your money.

In this email there will be instructions on where you want the FC Exchange to send the currency you have purchased; For example, I sent AUD and needed it to be converted to Euros.

* * *

Dear Your name,

Thank you for booking your transaction with FC Exchange and please find your PDF confirmation attached. The exchange rate for this trade has been fixed and the transaction is contractual.

What to do next! (if you have not already done so):

1.   Make your payment to FC Exchange

The PDF confirmation attached contains the FC Exchange client bank account details (marked "Settlement Instructions") where you need to send your money. Cleared funds should reach us by the settlement date on the attached confirmation. Late payments may attract penalties. All payments made to us should be sent by electronic transfer as we do not accept cash or cheques.

2.   Instruct FC Exchange where to send the currency you have purchased

Please provide FC Exchange with your ONWARD Payment Instruction by logging into the FCE secure payment submission site (link below). The password required is: **Password No.** (Please note this password is case sensitive). Secure Payment Submission Site: www.securefcexchangepayments.com

This allows us to receive your instructions quickly and securely. The site provides prompts to aid completion, but should you wish to receive the form in another format or have any issue submitting it please contact us on 020 7989 0000.

Please send any payment enquiry emails directly to *payments@fcexchange.co.uk*

Clients warrant that no payments will be processed until we receive a completed FC Exchange Payment Instruction form and the client is responsible for completing this correctly, legibly and in full. We accept no liability whatsoever arising from clients returning incorrect, incomplete or illegible payment instruction forms.

Unless we require your onward payment instructions this email does not require confirmation or response as it is for the purpose of record only. If you cannot open the attachment, notify us immediately and we will send it in a different format for you.

Kind Regards,
Senior FX Broker

FC Exchange | Salisbury House | Finsbury Circus | London | EC2M 5QQ | UK
T: +44 (0)20 7989 0000 | F: +44 (0)20 7989 9999 |
W: fcexchange.co.uk

WE'RE NOT A BANK. Visit our new website and find out who we are: *www.fcexchange.co.uk*

FC Exchange is a trading name of Foreign Currency Exchange Limited. Foreign Currency Exchange Limited is a limited company registered in England and Wales. Registered office: 88 Wood Street, 10th Floor, London, EC2V 7RS. Registered number: 5452483. Foreign Currency Exchange Limited is authorised by the Financial Services Authority (No. 511266) under the Payment Service Regulations 2009 for the provision of payment services. H M Customs & Excise MLR No.12215508. Please note that Foreign Currency Exchange Limited may monitor email traffic data and also the content of email for the purposes of security and staff training.

This message contains confidential information and is intended only for **YOUR EMAIL ADDRESS** If you are not **YOUR EMAIL ADDRESS** you should not disseminate, distribute or copy this e-mail. Please notify *atl@ fcexchange.co.uk* immediately by e-mail if you have received this e-mail by mistake and delete this e-mail from your system. E-mail transmission cannot be guaranteed to be secure or error-free as information could be intercepted, corrupted, lost, destroyed, arrive late or incomplete, or contain viruses. Therefore neither Foreign Currency Exchange Limited nor Amber Lean accepts liability for any errors or omissions in the contents of this message, which arise as a result of e-mail transmission. If verification is required please request a hard-copy version. Neither Foreign Currency Exchange Limited nor any employees of Foreign Currency Exchange Limited offer financial advice, clients should rely solely on their own judgement and are fully responsible for the decision to trade. The views or opinions in this e-mail are entirely those of the sender and do not necessarily represent the views or position of Foreign Currency Exchange Limited.

* * *

You will then click on the *www.securepayments.com* where you will complete the sections with the information of the person, the bank account numbers you wish to have the money sent to, and the currency.

Once you have completed the secure payment form and sent it, you should then receive the following email:

* * *

Dear Miss/Mrs/Mr _____,

This email is to confirm that we have received your Onward Payment Instruction Form via the FCE secure payment submission site. Your instruction will now be handed over to the payments team for processing.*

Kind Regards,

Please note we process payments on the same day that funds are received subject to funds being with us and fully cleared before 14:30hrs GMT. If we receive funds after this time, payments will be processed the following working day. We will only process your payment when the funds you send us are fully cleared. Next-day value or exotic currencies may require an additional clearing day due to time-differences and counter party delivery value. If you have any further payment queries in relation to clearance, delivery value and cut off times please contact your FC Exchange broker directly.

FC Exchange
FC Exchange | Salisbury House | Finsbury Circus | London | EC2M 5QQ
T: | F: +44 (0)20 7989 9999 | W: *fcexchange.co.uk*

Register with us: <u>open a free account</u> Help a friend save on their transfers: <u>refer a friend to FC Exchange</u>

FC Exchange is a trading name of Foreign Currency Exchange Limited. Foreign Currency Exchange Limited is a limited company registered in England and Wales. Registered office: Salisbury House, Finsbury Circus, London, EC2M 5QQ. Registered number: 5452483. Foreign Currency Exchange Limited is authorised by the Financial Conduct Authority (No. 511266) under the Payment Service Regulations 2009 for the provision of payment services. H M Customs & Excise MLR No.12215508. Please note that Foreign Currency Exchange Limited may monitor email traffic data and also the content of email for the purposes of security and staff training.

This message contains confidential information and is intended only for **YOUR EMAIL ADDRESS** If you are not **YOUR EMAIL ADDRESS** you should not disseminate, distribute or copy this e-mail. Please notify *info@fcexchange.co.uk* immediately by e-mail if you have received this e-mail by mistake and delete this e-mail from your system. E-mail transmission cannot be guaranteed to be secure or error-free as information could be intercepted, corrupted, lost, destroyed, arrive late or incomplete, or contain viruses. Therefore neither Foreign Currency Exchange Limited nor FC Exchange accepts liability for any errors or omissions in the contents of this message, which arise as a result of e-mail transmission. If verification is required please request a hard-copy version. Neither Foreign Currency Exchange Limited nor any employees of Foreign Currency Exchange Limited offer financial advice, clients should rely solely on their own judgement and are fully responsible for the decision to trade. The views or opinions in this e-mail are entirely those of the sender and do not necessarily represent the views or position of Foreign Currency Exchange Limited.

* * *

By the following day, you will receive a confirmation of transfer email as follows:

* * *

Dear Miss/Mrs/Mr,

Please find attached your Confirmation of Transfer document evidencing funds remitted on your behalf. If you have any questions, please contact us on 020 7989 0000 and we will be happy to help.

Please note the amount indicated on the attached document is the amount FC Exchange has sent, any discrepancy between this and the amount credited should first be addressed with the recipient bank as some banks may levy a receiving or routing charge.

Thank you for using FC Exchange.

Kind Regards,
Payments Co-ordinator

FCExchange | 10thFloor | 88WoodStreet | London | EC2V7RS
T: +44 (0)20 7989 0000 | F: +44 (0)20 7989 9999

FC Exchange is a trading name of Foreign Currency Exchange Limited. Foreign Currency Exchange Limited is a limited company registered in England and Wales. Registered office: 88 Wood

* * *

Attached to this email is a receipt, listing all the information that you sent through on the secure payments form, stating the date and time the money was received by the account you listed.

Please bear in mind that the more money you send directly through the FC Exchange to convert, the better rate you will get.

Also, for your information, if you refer someone to the FC Exchange you will be entitled to a £50 bonus payment per client – see below:

Referral information: FC Exchange client referral offer - If you know of someone, a friend, family member, anyone really that has or will have a foreign currency requirement, you can refer them to FC Exchange and as a thank you we'll give you £50.00.

Not only will you be rewarded, but the person you refer to FC Exchange will too. Obviously they'll benefit from our great rates and service but we'll also give them something to welcome them on board too.

So, how does it work? Simple really, ask the person you're referring to contact us and **quote reference CR814.**

Once they have registered and traded* with us, we'll credit £50.00 into your account here. It is as simple as that.

The small print and details

The referred client needs to trade a *minimum of £1,000.00 or FX equivalent in a single transaction. You do not need to be a client to refer someone to FC Exchange, but will need to be one to receive the £50.00.

The trading account of those referred will be credited with £10.00 on completion of their first trade with FC Exchange.

FC Exchange will need to know the details of the referring party for either party to benefit from the scheme; the onus is on the referrer or the referred to supply this information.

FC Exchange reserves the right to change the terms of this offer or to withdraw it at any time without notice or liability.

A maximum of £60.00 will be credited per new person or entity introduced. Any client already in touch with FC Exchange is not classed as a valid referral.

STEP 13

LIST OF ALL FEES AND CHARGES THAT ARE TO BE PAID BY THE BUYER

There are a number of costs involved in purchasing a property in Portugal, beginning with the following but not in the exact order:

1. **Fiscal Representation:** In obtaining a Fiscal Number I went with my advogado. You can go with your advogado or with someone you know who is fluent in Portuguese.

2. **Solicitor Fees:** The basic fees for an advogado to act as your legal representative are an estimated 250.00 €.

    All legal firms have a list of fees and some advogados charge much higher.

    In my case I paid 1,200.00 €, which I later found out was way too expensive.

    You can go online or in person to the Portuguese Law Society Bar Association and request a list of set minimum prices that an advogado can charge.

    Website and directory addresses for all Adgovados in Portugal;

    https://www.oa.pt/CD/Servicos/PesqAdvogados/pesquisa_adv. aspx?sidc=31634&idc=5&idsc=31897

    Keeping in mind, some advogados are not as honourable as others and if you're a foreigner they may charge you an exorbitant amount of money in some cases.

    The first advogado I contacted wanted to charge me 100 € an hour. I quickly left and said thank you very much but no thanks. They don't even charge that in Australia, where it costs between $600 AUD and $850 AUD to purchase a property.

    When I was charged 1,200 €, I questioned my advogado at the time, but I was told that is the normal price and that my contract was very complicated due to the lien, two (2) mortgages against the property and the way in which I wanted to structure the three payments to purchase the property.

I took it on good faith that the advogado was doing right by me and would not rip me off.

I also asked other owners, both Portuguese and foreigners in Portugal; most told me they couldn't remember what they had paid and some had inherited their property through their family.

When I found out from my current advogado firm that my fees should have only been 250 € I was not happy. I was so disappointed that I had been lied to and an easy target because I was a foreigner.

It was a lesson learned that I will never forget, as at the time it was an extra expense/burden on my finances. I think it is the general belief that, as foreigners, we can afford to pay more.

Some will advise that the cost of legal fees is roughly estimated at 1-2% of the purchase price of the property, plus VAT (in Australia we call it GST, which is a government tax).

3. **Purchase Tax:** This is called IMT and is known as Imposto Municipal Sorbre Transmissoes Onerosas de Imovies; this is the purchase tax that you pay when buying a property. It is paid by the buyer when a property is deeded/transferred into your name. The percentage paid depends on the registered use of the property that you have bought.

    I now believe that the original advogado I used did not look after my interests regarding this matter.

    After I bought the property, I was informed by my advogado that the property could bring in a number of incomes as it had multiple uses, so I needed to pay over 5,000 € in IMT fees.

I had already paid 65,000 €. I was being told by both my advogado and the real estate agent that it would be around 0.2% of the purchase price.

I was truly not very happy with another fee that was a huge expense and burden, especially as the Australian dollar was not doing too well against the Euro at the time.

4. **Land Registry Fees:** These fees are 0.5% of the purchase price.

5. **Property Registration Fees:** Your advogado will register your purchase of the property with the Property Registry Office (Consevatoria do Registo Predial) in the area where your property is located and at the Taxation Office (Reparticao de Financas).

6. **Registration of purchase** is fixed at 250 €

7. **Registration of mortgage** is fixed at 250 € if you are taking a mortgage through a bank to purchase the property.

8. **Stamp Duty** (Imposto de Selo) is 0.8% of the purchase price of the property.

9. **Notary Fees:** When the Notarial profession was privatised, notary fees changed significantly and now depend on the office where the Escritura is signed.

    The Escritura Pública de Compra e Venda (to give it the full name) has to be drawn up, signed by both parties in front of a public notary and lodged at the local Land Registry (Conservatoria do Registo Predial), with copies issued to the involved parties.

10. **VAT or IVA:** Is 23% on all new properties.

11. **Estate Agent's Fees:** These are paid by the vendor.

12. **Rates:** Paid quarterly or in one annual lump sum. You can set this up so that it is an automatic direct debit from your bank.

13. **Property Insurance:** An annual expense you need to pay, especially if you have a mortgage, in case of fire, burglary or damage. You will need to find an insurance company in Portugal for your policy.

    The type of insurance you need will depend on how you intend to use your property.

    I believe it is better to shop around for the right insurance broker that will cater to your exact needs. This you can do easily online, through any internet search engine.

CHECKLIST OF FEES THAT MAY BE CHARGED DURING THE PURCHASE OF A PROPERTY IN PORTUGAL

LIST	FEES	PAID
Fiscal Number	€	
Fiscal Representation	€	
Advogado/Advogada	€	
IMT –Purchase Tax	€	
Land Registry Fees	€	
Property Registration Fees	€	
Registration of Purchase	€	
Registration of Mortgage	€	
Stamp Duty Imposto de Selo	€	
Notary Fees	€	
VAT	€	
IVA	€	
Rates	€	
Property Insurance	€	

CHECKLISTS
STEP 1 – STEP 13

STEP 1 - ORGANISE FINANCE

FINANCE	DETAILS	COMPLETED
Personal:		
Mortgage: Contract:		
Swap: Contract:		
Rent/Buy: Contract:		
Owner Finance: Contract:		

STEP 2 – PROPERTY LOCATED

PROPERTY	DETAILS	COMPLETED
District:		
Municipality:		
Parish:		
Province:		
Region:		

STEP 3 – REAL ESTATE AGENT

AGENCY	DETAILS	COMPLETED
Company:		
Contact:		
Mobile:		
Address:		
Internet Address:		

STEP 4 – GOVERNMENT AUCTIONS

AUCTION	DETAILS	COMPLETED
Government Auction Reference No:		
Closed Letter:		
Online:		
Contract Submitted:		
Private Negotiation:		
Auction Dates:		
15 Days:		
20 Days:		
1/3 Deposit:	€	
2/3 Deposit:	€	
Remainder Deposit 8 Months:	€	
Imposto do Selo receipt no:		
Auto de Adjudicacao – Bill of Sale no:		

STEP 5 – BANK PROPERTIES

BANK	DETAILS	COMPLETED
Bank:		
Auctioneers:		
Address:		
Internet Address:		
Reference No:		
Deposit Paid:	€	
Receipt No:		

STEP 6 – PROMISSORY CONTRACT/CONTRACT OF SALE

Promissory Contract – Contract of Sale	DETAILS	COMPLETED
Casa Pronta Office: Contact Person:		
Advogado/Advogada Details:		
Construction Company:		
Real Estate Agent:		
Private Sale Details:		
Documents Translated:		

STEP 7 – LEGAL REPRESENTATION

LEGAL REPRESENTATION	DETAILS	COMPLETED
Company: Website Address:		
Advogado/Advogada Details:		
Landline: Mobile:		
Address:		

STEP 8 – FISCAL NUMBER

FISCAL NUMBER	DETAILS	COMPLETED
Identify Nearest Office:		
Address:		
Form Completed		
Tax File Number Documentation from home country		
Person 1 Name: Address: Date of Birth: Fiscal No: Country Tax File No: Email Address:		
Person 2 Name: Address: Date of Birth: Fiscal No: Country Tax File No: Email Address:		

STEP 9 – POWER OF ATTORNEY

POWER OF ATTORNEY	DETAILS	COMPLETED
Name of the person who has Power of Attorney:		
Address:		
Email Address:		
Contact Numbers:		
Powers:		
Electricity:		
Gas:		
Water:		
Property Insurance:		
Rates:	€	
Other:		

STEP 10 – NOTARY

NOTARY	DETAILS	COMPLETED
Name of the Notary:		
Address:		
Email Address:		
Contact Numbers:		
Witness 1: Name: Address: Contact Numbers: Email Address:		
Witness 2: Name: Address: Contact Numbers: Email Address:		
Notary Fees/Charges:	€	
Notary Receipt No:		

STEP 11 – LIENS & MORTGAGES ON THE PROPERTY

LIENS & MORTGAGES	DETAILS	COMPLETED
LIENS	€	
MORTGAGE	€	
SECOND MORTGAGE	€	
OWNERS		
LEGAL ACTIONS AGAINST THE PROPERTY		

LIST OF DOCUMENTS NEEDED TO
BUY AND SELL PROPERTY IN PORTUGAL

DOCUMENTS	DETAILS	COMPLETED
Seller and Buyer ID's / Passport (individuals)		
Commercial Certificate, representative ID, Pact of the Society (companies)		
Fiscal Number (Tax file number, see page 113)		
Power of attorney and ID of the procurator in case of use of a procurator		
Actual Land Carnet or Certificate of the Article content		
Certificate content descriptions and registrations in effect (or code to access)		
License of use in case of urban property, or certificate proving that your presentation is dispensed because it was built before August 7, 1951		
Demonstrating guide payment of Stamp Tax Transmissions and Municipal Tax (IMT)		
Technical description of the property (buildings after 2004)		
Energy certificate (This will be provided to you by the real estate agent or seller of the property)		

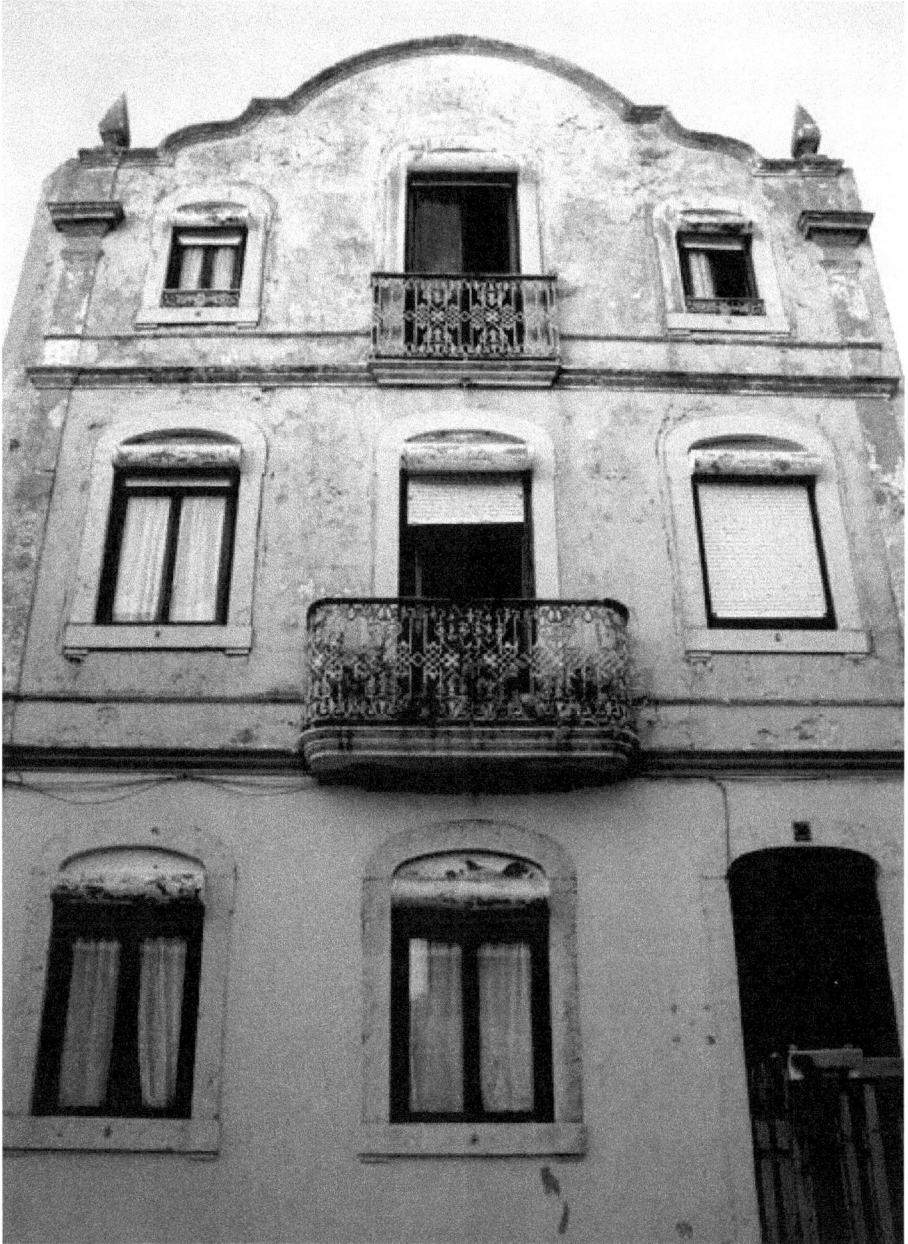

Before Photo: *I paid 65,000.00 € for this property;*
it comprised of 2 x 2 bedroom apartments,
1 x 3 bedroom apartment and 1 x 5 bedroom apartment.

After Photo: *Renovations are still ongoing.*

MISCELLANEOUS INFORMATION

For your information, if you are a foreigner in Portugal and are thinking of settling in Portugal, listed below are the:

TOP NATIONALITIES IN PORTUGAL

1. Americans in Portugal
2. Argentinians in Portugal
3. Australians in Portugal
4. Belgians in Portugal
5. Brazilians in Portugal
6. British in Portugal
7. Bulgarians in Portugal
8. Canadians in Portugal
9. Chinese in Portugal
10. Danish in Portugal
11. Dutch in Portugal
12. Finnish in Portugal
13. French in Portugal
14. Germans in Portugal
15. Greeks in Portugal
16. Indians in Portugal
17. Irish in Portugal
18. Italians in Portugal
19. Japanese in Portugal
20. Lebanese in Portugal
21. Mexicans in Portugal

22. Norwegians in Portugal
23. Polish in Portugal
24. Romanians in Portugal
25. Russians in Portugal
26. South Africans in Portugal
27. Spanish in Portugal
28. Swedish in Portugal
29. Swiss in Portugal
30. Turkish in Portugal
31. Ukrainians in Portugal

If you go to *www.expat.com* you can sign up to the Expat Community in Portugal, where you will be able to contact other foreigners, and perhaps fellow countrymen, who are living in Portugal.

The Expat Community is a wealth of information that can assist you in many areas. You can ask advice, join community groups and socialise.

CONCLUSION

You do not need to use the legal services of an advogado at all; as long as you are thorough in the processes I have listed, you should have no problems in purchasing a property in Portugal.

It is your choice if you wish to use an advogado, utilise the services of the real estate agent or do it yourself through the Casa Pronta office, between just the seller and yourself.

Real Estate agents can do just about all the work for you, regarding everything from the Fiscal Number and the Notary to connecting the electricity, gas and water. They can make an appointment to go to the Casa Pronta office or the Notary Office.

There are so many simple ways to purchase a property in Portugal; you have to decide which way you want to go about it. As a foreigner, I was taken advantage of and overcharged in the process. I do not wish this to happen to any other person who wants to purchase a property in Portugal.

Putting that aside, I still believe that Portugal is an untapped market and has huge potential, especially for foreigners.

In Australia, property is so expensive and it is extremely hard to find a property under $100,000 AUD. You are looking at a minimum of $300,000 AUD for a simple 3 bedroom house; even then it is very hard to find one for that price.

The fact is that you can buy property at affordable prices in Portugal; even if you have to renovate the property, it is still so much cheaper and simplier to buy in Portugal than most other countries.

The feeling you get, when you can just pay cash for a property and not have to take out a mortgage, is indescribable.

The joy and inner peace you feel when you have a home and the bonus of not having to pay thousands of dollars per year in rent or mortgage, is priceless.

You have to determine what you want out of life, what makes you happy and how & where you wish to live your life.

Whether you choose to purchase a property in Portugal for retirement, as an investment or to make a complete life change, it is your decision. For me, it has been the best decision of my life and I cannot wait to live there full time.

The main purpose of this book is to outline the very basics in buying a property in Portugal; the book can be used as a guideline for anyone wanting to purchase a property.

All information I have provided I have used in buying my own property, I have found online, researched and is true and correct as of 2015.

Thank you very much and I hope this books helps all those looking to buy a property in Portgual.